NINETEENTH-CENTURY
SAINTS
AT WAR

NINETEENTH-CENTURY SAINTS AT WAR

Edited by

ROBERT C. FREEMAN

RELIGIOUS STUDIES CENTER
BRIGHAM YOUNG UNIVERSITY

Front cover: *Utah Light Artillery*, by Keith Rocco. Courtesy of Utah National Guard.

Back cover: An artillery shell explodes near one of the Utah Battery's positions. Photo courtesy of Church Archives.

Published by the Religious Studies Center, Brigham Young University, Provo, Utah
© 2007 by Brigham Young University
All rights reserved

Any uses of this material beyond those allowed by the exemptions in U.S. copyright law, such as section 107, "Fair Use," and section 108, "Library Copying," require the written permission of the publisher, Religious Studies Center, 167 HGB, Brigham Young University, Provo, Utah 84602. The views expressed herein are the responsibility of the individual authors and do not necessarily represent the position of Brigham Young University or the Religious Studies Center.

ISBN-13   978-0-8425-2694-4

To All Generations
of Latter-day Saints at War

★ ★ ★

I RECENTLY FINISHED READING the book *1776*, by renowned scholar and historian David McCullough. It was an inspiring opportunity to relive the American Revolution. Going into the experience, I anticipated an excellent treatment on the strategies of war, the great battles fought, and the key moments of victory and defeat during the Revolution. I was not as prepared for the emotional journey that this book would take me on as I felt so much of the agony and suffering of war. I didn't anticipate the poignant feelings I would have towards that brave generation of patriots. It deepened my feelings of love for my country and for freedom. Who would say that those who fought in that war were not members of a greatest generation—just as Tom Brokaw dubbed the World War II generation. For that matter, could it not be said of any generation where soldiers of any nation fought for the protection or extension of freedom they too should be remembered as a greatest generation?

Prior to his passing, I had the privilege of interviewing Elder Neal A. Maxwell of the Quorum of the Twelve Apostles about his wartime experiences as a youth in World War II. When I asked him if his was the greatest generation, he turned back the compliment, labeling the title as "praise too effusive." When pressed to name a greatest generation, he suggested that perhaps the generation of youth of our day could be that greatest generation. So to the Latter-day Saint soldier in every conflict of the past who answered the call of their country to assist in preserving freedom—thank you. To those of the generations going forward who may yet be called upon to defend our freedoms, we say thank you ahead of time. God bless the faithful soldier whose defense of freedom is placed ahead of the preservation of his own life.

Contents

✶ ✶ ✶

Acknowledgments ix

1 "Renounce War and Proclaim Peace": Early Beginnings 1
    ANDREW C. SKINNER

  Introduction to the Mexican-American War.......................... 35
2 The Church and the Mexican-American War 41
    LARRY C. PORTER

  Introduction to the Utah War 77
3 The Church and the Utah War, 1857–58.............................. 81
    SHERMAN L. FLEEK

  Introduction to the Civil War... 107
4 The Church and the Civil War... 113
    DAVID F. BOONE

  Introduction to the Spanish-American and
  Philippine Wars 151
5 The Spanish-American and Philippine Wars........................ 155
    JAMES I. MANGUM

  Index 195

Acknowledgments

✶ ✶ ✶

WE ARE DEEPLY INDEBTED to each author who contributed to this volume. All have contributed to present important perspectives in the areas of their individual expertise. Each has produced a scholarly yet faithful treatment of his subject. In the editing process, every effort has been made to retain the message of each author while dealing with sometimes sensitive issues which the topic of war is inclined to produce. Each author has been flexible and supportive in this regard. We hope that the product of this collaborative effort will be a volume that can fill a useful niche in Latter-day Saint historical literature.

Sincere thanks are expressed to the Religious Studies Center at Brigham Young University. Led by Dr. Richard Holzapfel, this team of professionals includes Devan Jensen, Joany Pinegar, and bright student researchers and others who have greatly assisted in bringing this work to completion. Thanks, too, for the services of Dr. Don Norton, professor emeritus at BYU, for his careful review of much of this volume. An expert in veteran research, Don has contributed much to the research efforts of the *Saints at War* project. We are also grateful to the administration of Religious Education and the Department of Church History and Doctrine for their ongoing support of such research activities as the *Saints at War* project.

Gratitude is also extended to the fine students of the *Saints at War* research staff who have labored so ably to assist in the exhaustive research, writing, and compilation efforts related to this book. Included in this group of contributors are Ryan Aldredge, Jessica Brown, Jenny Curlee, Jon Felt, Robert Hall, Jeff Jenson, Marianne Myers, Zach Smith, Jason Thompson, Brian Warburton, Eliot Wilcox, Chris Winters, Paola Velez, and Mike Winchester.

Much of the source information and factual background for introductions to chapters and some sidebars were drawn from John Whiteclay Chambers II, ed., *The Oxford Companion to American Military History* (New York: Oxford University Press, 1999). Finally, thanks to Dr. Dennis Wright, cofounder of the *Saints at War* project. His energy and ability have shaped so much of the success of the research inspiring this volume.

1

"Renounce War and Proclaim Peace": Early Beginnings

ANDREW C. SKINNER

WAR IS A COMPLEX ISSUE—socially, politically, economically, and religiously. However, members of The Church of Jesus Christ of Latter-day Saints can rely on clearly articulated doctrines and principles as they seek to formulate their own stance on armed conflict in general and on specific wars in particular. These inspired and inspiring principles issue from the Lord Himself through the standard works and the published words of prophets and apostles in this last dispensation.

Andrew C. Skinner is director of the Neal A. Maxwell Institute for Religious Scholarship at Brigham Young University.

"There was war in heaven: Michael and his angels fought against the dragon" (Revelation 11:7). *The Archangel Michael*, painting by Guido Reni. Courtesy of Bridgeman-Giraudon/Art Resource, NY.

Origins and Nature of War

War has taken many lives and has caused much misery in this fallen world. As President Thomas S. Monson lamented, "The cruelty of war seems to bring forth hatred toward others and disregard for human life."[1] But, significantly, war is not unique to mortality. It existed in our premortal life. Its author was Lucifer, or Satan, an angel in authority in the presence of God who rebelled against Him (see D&C 76:25). As a result of Satan's arrogant obstinacy, "there was war in heaven: Michael and his angels fought against the dragon; and the dragon fought and his angels. . . . And the great dragon was cast out [of heaven], that old serpent, called the Devil, and Satan, which deceiveth the whole world: he was cast out into the earth, and his angels were cast out with him" (Revelation 12:7, 9).

The War in Heaven was fought over the foundational issues of eternity: who would be the earth-born Savior of humankind, how salvation would be gained, and whether or not agency would be preserved. Lucifer sought to destroy the agency of humankind and to usurp the kingdom of the Father and the Son. He and "a third part" of our Heavenly Father's spirit children rejected Jesus Christ and His Atonement. They were thrust out of the Father's presence, cast down to earth without the possibility of gaining mortal bodies, and so became the devil and his angels (see D&C 76:25–28; 29:36–37; Moses 4:1–4).

Latter-day revelation given through the Prophet Joseph Smith unequivocally declares that Satan transferred to this earth the war he began in heaven, causing great misery. "Wherefore, he maketh war with the saints of God, and encompasseth them round about. And we saw a vision of the sufferings of those with whom he made war and overcame, for thus came the voice of the Lord unto us" (D&C 76:29–30). John the Revelator also testified that "it was given unto him [Satan] to make war with the saints" in this mortal realm

(Revelation 13:7). In our day, President Gordon B. Hinckley, speaking after the terrorist attacks of September 11, 2001, said: "Now, all of us know that war, contention, hatred, suffering of the worst kind are not new. The conflict we see today is but another expression of the conflict that began with the War in Heaven."[2]

Warfare is endemic to mortality. It has been with us as long as Satan has been.

Thus, warfare in mortality is actually the earthly manifestation of the war inaugurated in our premortal existence, with all of its ensuing misery, sorrow, and destruction—horrendous destruction. In fact, for his rebellion and unrelenting prosecution of war against agency, Satan himself was called "Perdition" (D&C 76:26), meaning utter destruction, complete ruin or loss. He is the personification of complete ruin. He is the personification of war. Therefore, how can we expect that war will produce anything but destruction? And it should come as no surprise that the fundamental principle of agency is almost always at the heart of earthly armed conflict between those who support its expansion and those who press for its contraction.

Again, President Hinckley said, "War, of course, is not new. The weapons change. The ability to kill and destroy is constantly refined. But there has been conflict throughout the ages *over essentially the same issues.*"[3]

Warfare, then, is endemic to mortality. It has been with us as long as Satan has been. It is so much a part of the history of this world that John the Revelator used the images and symbols of war to summarize and characterize this earth's temporal history, as portrayed in six one-thousand-year periods called seals (see D&C 77:7). In John's scheme, the horse, the bow, and the sword all symbolize war—war that Satan has unleashed and fostered in this world (see Revelation 6:1–9; 9:16–17). And, of course, the culminating event preparatory to the Second Coming of Jesus Christ is Armageddon—a battle so sweeping and horrendous that "all nations" will be gathered together to fight against Jerusalem (see Zechariah 12–14; Revelation 16:14–21).

But even the Second Coming does not end the horror of war once and for all. After the Millennium, Satan "shall be loosed for a little season, that he may gather together his armies. And Michael, the seventh angel, even the archangel, shall gather together his armies, even the hosts of heaven. And the devil shall gather together his armies; even the hosts of hell, and shall come up to battle against Michael and his armies. And then cometh the battle of the great God; and the devil and his armies shall be cast away into their own place, that they shall not have power over the saints any more at all. For Michael shall fight their battles, and shall overcome him who seeketh the throne of him who sitteth upon the throne, even the Lamb" (D&C 88:111–15).

Hence we see that, ironically, warfare and the plan of salvation (or great plan of happiness) are inextricably tied together. This does not mean, however, that God relishes or even approves of war. But He does possess a particular view about it.

The Lord's View

On August 6, 1833, the Lord revealed anew His overarching perspective on war. Known as Doctrine and Covenants 98, the revelation came to Joseph Smith in Kirtland, Ohio, as a result of the persecution being heaped upon the Saints in Missouri. Having suffered physically and emotionally, and having lost property as a consequence of the adversary's war against the Church of Jesus Christ, it was only natural that the Missouri members "should

C. C. A. Christensen (1831–1912), *Saints Driven from Jackson County, Missouri*, ca. 1865, tempera on muslin, 77 ¼ x 113 inches. Courtesy of Brigham Young University Museum of Art. All rights reserved.

feel an inclination toward retaliation and revenge."[4] But the Lord asked for and outlined something different. From the words of the revelation, it is clear that these principles extend to all the Lord's people across every dispensation. The Lord called these principles "an ensample unto all people" (D&C 98:38).

First, the Lord declared that His Saints are to "renounce war and proclaim peace" (D&C 98:16). Instead of seeking war, they are to "seek diligently to turn the hearts of the children to their fathers, and the hearts of the fathers to the children" (D&C 98:16). In other words, true Saints of the Lord's kingdom are asked to search first for peaceful solutions to problems that could be dealt with violently. They are to counter the destructive forces of war by living the gospel covenant and by establishing eternal links and bonds between generations through priesthood ordinances that can seal together the entire human family—the family of God. God asks that His children be bound together rather than torn apart. The power to counter the destructive forces of war and establish God's kingdom throughout the world is as real as the power that is unleashed in armed conflict. But the capacity to harness that power is predicated upon righteous living and intense, sustained effort to prepare for and establish peace.

It is doubtful that as much effort has ever been expended in proclaiming peace as it has been in promoting war. President Spencer W. Kimball rebuked the world when he stated:

> We are a warlike people, easily distracted from our assignment of preparing for the coming of the Lord. When enemies rise up, we commit vast resources to the fabrication of gods of stone and steel—ships, planes, missiles, fortifications—and depend on them for protection and deliverance. When threatened, we become antienemy instead of pro-kingdom of God; we train a man in the art of war and call him a patriot, thus, in the manner of Satan's counterfeit of true patriotism, perverting the Savior's teaching: "Love your enemies, bless them that curse you, do good to them that hate you, and pray for them which despitefully use you, and persecute you. That ye may be the children of your Father which is in heaven" (Matthew 5:44–45).[5]

Warfare is fundamentally incongruous with the Lord's nature and personality. For example, in ancient Israel, King David was forbidden to build a permanent temple of the Lord in Jerusalem because of his involvement in much warfare: "But the word of the Lord came to me, saying, Thou hast shed blood abundantly, and hast made great wars: thou shalt not build an house unto my name, because thou hast shed much blood upon the earth in my sight" (1 Chronicles 22:8). War and bloodshed take their toll on individuals and on nations. Warriors who survive armed conflict are often those who bear the deepest wounds and scars of war. As a youth, David was characterized as being a man after the Lord's "own heart" (1 Samuel 13:14). But war desensitized and hardened David to the point that he killed Uriah the Hittite by sending him to "the forefront of the hottest battle" (2 Samuel 11:15) to cover up his adultery with Bathsheba, Uriah's wife.

President David O. McKay stated what others have said—that "war is incompatible with Christ's teachings" and that "it is vain to attempt to reconcile war with true Christianity."[6] The ancient seer Enoch beheld wondrous visions of the first and second comings of the Prince of Peace. He taught the gospel of Jesus Christ, walked with God, and "was before his face *continually*" (D&C 107:49; emphasis added). But perhaps most touching and telling is his personal witness of God weeping over man's horrible treatment of his fellowman: "And it came to pass that the God of heaven looked upon the residue of the people, and he wept; and Enoch bore record of it, saying: How is it that the heavens weep, and shed forth their tears as the rain upon the mountains? And Enoch said unto the Lord: How is it that thou canst weep seeing thou art holy, and from all eternity to all eternity? . . . The Lord said unto Enoch: . . . Unto thy brethren have I said, and also given commandment, that they should love one another, and that they should choose me, their Father; but behold, they are without affection, and they hate their own blood" (Moses 7:28–29, 32–33).

War is a manifestation of that hatred and malice. It pains God deeply, and He has counseled against war in very strong terms. Still, the Lord does not refuse to tutor and counsel His children when war does break out. Although He teaches the ideal ("renounce war and proclaim peace," D&C 98:16), He understands human nature and knows that war is sometimes unavoidable, precisely because Satan seeks to overthrow the kingdom of God by inciting war. God knows that men use the very agency He provided them in order to reject Him and His beneficent plan. But He never ceases to call, persuade, direct aright, and give guidance to His followers.

> "There are times and circumstances when nations are justified . . . to fight for family, for liberty, and against tyranny."

Thus, a second part of the Lord's doctrine of war that has broad application comprises a policy of what might be termed "defensive war." The Lord exhorts His covenant peoples to bear patiently the attacks inflicted upon them by their enemies (see D&C 98:23–27) and "not go out unto battle against any nation, kindred, tongue, or people" unless He commands it (D&C 98:33). "There are times and circumstances," said President Hinckley, "when nations are justified, in fact have an obligation, to fight for family, for liberty, and against tyranny, threat, and oppression."[7] Throughout the ages, God has commanded and inspired righteous people to resist tyranny and oppression and fight for family and liberty. Who can doubt that Captain Moroni was so inspired? He scrupulously adhered to the Lord's doctrine of defensive warfare, believing "that God would make it known unto them whither they should go to defend themselves against their enemies, and by so doing, the Lord would deliver them; and this was the faith of Moroni, and his heart did glory in it; not in the shedding of blood but in doing good, in preserving his people, yea, in keeping the commandments of God, yea, and resisting iniquity" (Alma 48:16).

Moroni is the model—the personification—of President Hinckley's teachings on the nature of divinely approved warfare.

Captain Moroni Raises the Title of Liberty, Arnold Friberg ©1951 IRI.

He did not glory in the shedding of blood. Nevertheless, there came a time when Moroni "rent his coat; and he took a piece thereof, and wrote upon it—In memory of our God, our religion, and freedom, and our peace, our wives, and our children—and he fastened it upon the end of a pole. And he fastened on his head-plate, and his breastplate and his shields, and girded on his armor about his loins; and he took the pole, which had on the end thereof his rent coat, (and he called it the title of liberty) and he bowed himself to the earth, and he prayed mightily unto his God for the blessings of liberty to rest upon his brethren, so long as there should a band of Christians remain to possess the land" (Alma 46:12–13).

In what has become a classic statement on war, President David O. McKay also explained that there are conditions and reasons which justify Christian disciples in taking up arms against an opposing force:

> Such a condition, however, is not a real or fancied insult given by one nation to another. When this occurs proper reparation may be made by mutual understanding, apology, or by arbitration.
>
> Neither is there justifiable cause found in a desire or even a need for territorial expansion. The taking of territory implies the subjugation of the weak by the strong.
>
> Nor is war justified in an attempt to enforce a new order of government, or even to impel others to a particular form of worship, however better the government or eternally true the principles of the enforced religion may be. . . .
>
> There are, however, two conditions which may justify a truly Christian man to enter—*enter, not begin*—a war: (1) An attempt by others to dominate and to deprive another of his free agency, and (2) Loyalty to his own country. Possibly there is a third, viz., Defense of a weak nation that is being unjustly crushed by a strong, ruthless one.
>
> Paramount among these reasons, of course, is the defense of man's freedom. To deprive an intelligent human being of his free agency is to commit the crime of the ages. Without freedom of thought, freedom of choice, freedom of action within lawful

bounds, man cannot progress. Throughout the ages, advanced souls have yearned for a society in which liberty and justice prevail. Men have sought for it, fought for it, have died for it. Ancient freemen prized it, slaves longed for it, the Magna Carta demanded it, the Constitution of the United States declared it.

A second obligation that impels us to become participants in war is loyalty to government. The greatest responsibility of the state is to guard the lives and to protect the property and rights of its citizens; and if the state is obligated to protect its citizens from lawlessness within its boundaries, it is equally obligated to protect them from lawless encroachments from without—whether the attacking criminals be individuals or nations. The state is duty bound to protect itself against treachery, and its only effective means of doing so under present world conditions is by armed force.[8]

God as Divine Warrior

Illustrating and emphasizing the constancy of the Lord's position on war, Doctrine and Covenants 98 is actually a recapitulation of the law of warfare He gave to "all [his] ancient prophets and apostles" (D&C 98:32). He justified His covenant people in going to battle only *after* they had brought the matter before Him.

> Behold, this is the law I gave unto my servant Nephi, and thy fathers, Joseph, and Jacob, and Isaac, and Abraham, and all mine ancient prophets and apostles.
>
> And again, this is the law that I gave unto mine ancients, that they should not go out unto battle against any nation, kindred, tongue, or people, save I, the Lord, commanded them.
>
> And if any nation, tongue, or people should proclaim war against them, they should first lift a standard of peace unto that people, nation, or tongue;

And if that people did not accept the offering of peace, neither the second nor the third time, they should bring these testimonies before the Lord;

Then I, the Lord, would give unto them a commandment, and justify them in going out to battle against that nation, tongue, or people. (D&C 98:32–36)

The Lord then reminded the Saints of this dispensation that in ancient times, after sincere efforts at peace failed, He would fight His followers' battles for them, "and their children's battles, and their children's children's, until they had avenged themselves on all their enemies, to the third and fourth generation" (D&C 98:37). It is in this context that Exodus 15:3 is meant to be taken: "The Lord is a man of war: the Lord is his name." The Lord fights the battles of the righteous.

The same promise given to the ancients has been reissued to the Saints of the latter days. President Spencer W. Kimball stated:

We forget that if we are righteous the Lord will either not suffer our enemies to come upon us—and this is the special promise to the inhabitants of the land of the Americas (see 2 Ne. 1:7)—or he will fight our battles for us (Ex. 14:14; D&C 98:37, to name only two references of many). This he is able to do, for as he said at the time of his betrayal, "Thinkest thou that I cannot now pray to my Father, and he shall presently give me more than twelve legions of angels?" (Matt. 26:53.) We can imagine what fearsome soldiers they would be. King Jehoshaphat and his people were delivered by such a troop (see 2 Chr. 20), and when Elisha's life was threatened, he comforted his servant by saying, "Fear not: for they that be with us are more than they that be with them" (2 Kgs. 6:16). The Lord then opened the eyes of the servant, "And he saw: and, behold, the mountain was full of horses and chariots of fire round about Elisha" (2 Kgs. 6:17).

... What are we to fear when the Lord is with us? Can we not take the Lord at his word and exercise a particle of faith in him? Our assignment is affirmative: to forsake the things of the world as ends in themselves; to leave off idolatry and press forward in faith; to carry the gospel to our enemies, that they might no longer be our enemies.[9]

As President Kimball pointed out, there is overwhelming evidence showing that God does fight the battles and wars of His covenant followers. To the Israelites, who were facing the onslaught of the Egyptian army at the shores of the Red Sea, Moses declared, "Fear ye not, stand still, and see the salvation of the Lord, which he will shew to you to day: for the Egyptians whom ye have seen to day, ye shall see them again no more for ever. The Lord shall fight for you, and ye shall hold your peace" (Exodus 14:13–14). The Lord fulfilled His promise.

In Joshua's day, "the sun stood still, and the moon stayed, until the people had avenged themselves upon their enemies. . . . So the sun stood still in the midst of heaven, and hasted not to go down about a whole day. And there was no day like that before it or after it, that the Lord hearkened unto the voice of a man: for the Lord fought for Israel" (Joshua 10:13–14).

Through the prophet Isaiah, the Lord declared that He would defend Jerusalem, the city of His temple, against the attack of the Assyrians. And indeed He did!

> Therefore thus saith the Lord concerning the king of Assyria, He shall not come into this city, nor shoot an arrow there, nor come before it with shields, nor cast a bank against it.
>
> By the way that he came, by the same shall he return, and shall not come into this city, saith the Lord.
>
> For I will defend this city to save it for mine own sake, and for my servant David's sake.

> Then the angel of the Lord went forth, and smote in the camp of the Assyrians a hundred and fourscore and five thousand: and when they arose early in the morning, behold, they were all dead corpses.
>
> So Sennacherib king of Assyria departed, and went and returned, and dwelt at Nineveh. (Isaiah 37:33–37)

The foregoing are just a few of the many examples that can be drawn from ancient sources (modern ones exist as well) showing God's desire and capability to be King, Battle Master, Guardian, and Protector of His covenant people. Without question, sacred history has shown the Lord to be "a man of war" (Exodus 15:3). He has gone into battle to defend His people and further His purposes. And He has justified people in going to war over tyranny, oppression, and liberty. He may continue to do so. But here a huge caution must be reiterated: it is God's place to justify man in going to war and not man's place to justify self-determined involvement in war based on examples of God's fighting past battles. "Few armies in any century, and especially the twentieth, have gone to war without the conviction that their cause was somehow justifiable and even righteous. *Wehrmacht* soldiers of Hitler's conquering Third Reich wore the Motto 'Gott mit uns,' or 'God with us,' emblazoned on their belt buckles."[10] Human beings can deceive and be deceived. Only God is wholly righteous. Only He is master of justice and mercy. Only He can know all things, including the thoughts and intents of people's hearts (see D&C 6:16). Only He can weigh and evaluate with perfect understanding the merits of an action. Only He is or can be the perfect Judge in all matters. Only He has the wisdom and power to use war to further His eternal purposes. Decisions about war, including guiding principles, should be left to Him.

Prophets ancient and modern have spoken about, and provided examples of God using war to further His eternal purposes. These eternal purposes contrast with the sometimes short-sighted, impatient, more immediate focus of mortals. From personal experience President Ezra Taft Benson knew and testified that the Lord had "turned disasters—war, occupation, and revolution—into blessings."[11] By His intervention in the American Revolutionary War, the Lord turned what appeared to be certain disaster (for the colonists) into an amazing victory and a great blessing for the whole world. Though the war was bloody and destructive in its effects, miracle after miracle occurred on the North American continent during the war (1775–83) to establish political, religious, and economic freedom in America and thereby hold up a standard and an ensign for the rest of the world to rally around.

It was nothing but the intervention of God that snatched victory from the jaws of defeat. Weakness on the part of the colonists was one of the reasonable arguments of those who opposed a war against Britain. Indeed, on paper the colonies were no match against the motherland. They were anything but unified. The colonists had differing interests, economically and politically. Geographically they were stretched out 1,400 miles—from Maine to Georgia. They had no collective financial backing. In 1775 Great Britain had a standing army of fifty-five thousand and over two million men that could be called to arms. The colonies had an untrained militia of several thousand that were a ragtag assemblage of farmers, trappers, and entrepreneurs. Britain had the most powerful navy in the world. The colonies had no navy. Britain had thousands of armaments, rifles, and cannons. All the guns and powder the colonists had came from England.[12]

But the Lord moved into the conflict. His plans and maneuvers were unstoppable. France and Spain became "blind instruments *in the hands of providence* employed to aid in founding a nation which should cultivate those republican virtues that were destined yet to regenerate the world . . . and eventually to overthrow the timeworn system of tyrannical usurpation of the few over many."[13] The

General George Washington Receives a Salute on the Field of Trenton, 1776.
Courtesy of National Archives.

eyewitness testimony of George Washington regarding God's intervention is compelling. "It having pleased the Almighty Ruler of the Universe propitiously to defend the cause of the United American States . . . by raising up a powerful Friend among the Princes of the Earth to establish our liberty and Independence upon lasting foundations, it becomes us to set apart a day for gratefully acknowledging the divine Goodness, and celebrating the important Event which we owe to his benign interposition."[14]

The Revolutionary War suited God's purposes. He did not delight in the loss of life or limb, nor the shedding of blood, nor the destruction of lands and property. But the war suited His eternal purposes, and He turned it into an eternal blessing for all peoples. Out of the war came the United States Constitution, which "should be maintained for the rights and protection of all flesh, according to just and holy principles; that every man may act in doctrine and principle pertaining to futurity, according to the moral agency which I have given unto him, that every man may be accountable for his own sins in the day of judgment. Therefore, it is not right that any man should be in bondage one to another. And for this purpose have I established the Constitution of this land, by the hands of wise men whom I raised up unto this very purpose, and redeemed the land by the shedding of blood" (D&C 101:77–80).

> The Lord says He redeemed the land by the shedding of blood. Those patriots and colonists who lost their lives or shed their blood in the American Revolutionary War did so for a noble and eternal cause.

It is significant that the Lord says He redeemed the land by the shedding of blood. Those patriots and colonists who lost their lives or shed their blood in the American Revolutionary War did so for a noble and eternal cause. God turned that sacrifice into something that has benefited the human family for eternity. As President Joseph F. Smith noted: "This great American nation the Almighty raised up by the power of his omnipotent hand, that it might be possible in the latter days for the kingdom of God to be established in the earth. If the Lord had not prepared the way by laying the foundations of this glorious nation, it would have been impossible (under the stringent laws and bigotry of the monarchical governments of the world) to have laid the foundations for the coming of his great kingdom. *The Lord has done this.*"[15]

God uses the loss of life in warfare to further His eternal purposes and to bless those who perish. Moroni, prophet and captain of the guard, provided comfort to those who mourn the loss of loved ones in armed conflict. "For the Lord suffereth the righteous to be slain that his justice and judgment may come upon the wicked; therefore ye need not suppose that the righteous are lost because they are slain; but behold, they do enter into the rest of the Lord" (Alma 60:13).

Soon after the United States entered World War II, during the April general conference in 1942, Elder Harold B. Lee instructed the Saints:

> In this terrible war now waging, thousands of our righteous young men in all parts of the world and in many countries are subject to a call into the military service of their own countries. Some of these, so serving, have already been called back to their heavenly home; others will almost surely be called to follow. But "behold," as Moroni said, the righteous of them who serve and are slain "do enter into the rest of the Lord their God," [Alma 60:13] and of them the Lord has said "those that die in me shall not taste of death, for it shall be sweet unto them." (D.&C. 42:46) Their salvation and exaltation in the world to come will be secure. That in their work of destruction they will be striking at their brethren will not be held against them. That sin, as Moroni of old said, is to the condemnation of those who "sit in their places of power in

a state of thoughtless stupor," those rulers in the world who in a frenzy of hate and lust for unrighteous power and dominion over their fellow men, have put into motion eternal forces they do not comprehend and cannot control. God, in His own due time, will pass sentence upon them.[16]

At the very next conference, in October 1942, Elder Lee gave additional insight into why the righteous are sometimes slain in battle. He declared, "It is my conviction that the present devastating scourge of war in which hundreds of thousands are being slain, many of whom are no more responsible for the causes of the war than are our own boys, is making necessary an increase of missionary activity in the spirit world and that many of our boys who bear the Holy Priesthood and are worthy to do so will be called to that missionary service after they have departed this life."[17]

The Lord possesses an eternal perspective. Man usually possesses a restricted view. The Lord has all power and wisdom to accomplish His purposes, which are always in harmony with His work and His glory, "to bring to pass the immortality and eternal life of man" (Moses 1:39). Man possesses limited power and knowledge. We cannot see the end from the beginning in all things. It is both comforting and essential to remember, when talking about war, illness, or any of the many injustices or unfair aspects of life, that ultimately the Lord "doeth not anything save it be for the benefit of the world; for he loveth the world" (2 Nephi 26:24).

It is also in this telestial state of mortality that the Lord permits the existence of war and its attendant evils in order to have agency operate in our lives and to have the tests of daily living refine us as His disciples. The First Presidency again explained:

> God, doubtless, could avert war, prevent crime, destroy poverty, chase away darkness, overcome error, and make all things

bright, beautiful and joyful. But this would involve the destruction of a vital and fundamental attribute in man—the right of agency. It is for the benefit of His sons and daughters that they become acquainted with evil as well as good, with darkness as well as light, with error as well as truth, and with the results of the infraction of eternal laws. Therefore he has permitted the evils which have been brought about by the acts of His creatures, but will control their ultimate results for His own glory and the progress and exaltation of His sons and daughters, when they have learned obedience by the things they suffer.[18]

This Latter-day Dispensation

Because the Lord knows the end from the beginning (see Isaiah 46:10), His perspective on war is informed by all events past and future. Every era has witnessed wars and rumors of wars, but the Lord has taken particular care from the beginning of time to focus attention on the dispensation of the fullness of times and on the commotion and warfare that will engulf the world prior to His Second Coming. Prophecies about wars and destruction given in all previous dispensations ultimately funnel our attention toward these last days.

Enoch saw the wickedness, vengeance, and war that would be rampant on earth before the Second Coming (see Moses 7:59–67). Lehi and Nephi saw in vision the wars and rumors of wars that began to spread among all nations prior to the Restoration of the gospel and beyond (see 1 Nephi 14:16–17). During His earthly ministry, our Lord proclaimed that during the last days the earth's inhabitants would "hear of wars, and rumors of wars" before His return in glory (Joseph Smith—Matthew 1:28). And, finally, Joseph Smith began to comprehend early on in his ministry what the ancients knew: that beginning in his own time there would constantly be wars and rumors of wars until the end of the world (see D&C 45:26). He came to know that war would be poured out upon the earth because of the wickedness of people. The beginning of the end would be the American Civil War, commencing in South Carolina in 1861, and war would spread to all nations and would not cease until the coming of the Son of Man (see D&C 87).

Even before the revelations of March 7, 1831 (see D&C 45), and December 25, 1832 (see D&C 87), the Saints experienced conflicts and received revelations that began to help them understand the Lord's attitude toward war. In January 1831, as persecution toward the Church increased in New York, the Lord commanded the Saints to move west to Ohio in order to "escape the power of the enemy" (D&C 38:31). Rather than retaliate against or resist those promoting violence, the Lord told His people He wanted them gathered to Him "a righteous people, without spot and blameless" (D&C 38:31). Then He would give to them His law and endow them with "power from on high" (D&C 38:32). And so the New York Saints moved west to northern Ohio, ready to enjoy the promised endowments of knowledge and power from on high.

It is significant that the Lord prefaced His instruction regarding escape from enemy forces by chiding the Saints for focusing on the grand signs of the times, while being somewhat oblivious to the smaller, yet significant issues at home. "Ye hear of wars in far countries, and you say that there will soon be great wars in far countries, but ye know not the hearts of men in your own land" (D&C 38:29). From this comment, we know that the Saints were well aware of the latter-day prophecies regarding war, and were thinking about them.

The Kirtland period of Church history was one of unparalleled development. Priesthood organization, doctrinal restoration, glorious manifestations, and the members' spiritual education all issued from the Kirtland experience. Construction on this new

The Prophet Joseph Smith Jr., Alvin Gittens ©1959 IRI.

dispensation's first temple—the focal point of this era's pentecostal outpouring—began on June 6, 1833. But work on the temple again raised the specter of war against the Saints, and thus Kirtland also proved to be a period of significant persecution. "Mobs threatened to destroy the temple, and those who worked on it by day guarded it at night. Night after night for weeks, Heber C. Kimball said, we 'were not permitted to take off our clothes, and were obliged to lay with our fire locks in our arms.'"¹⁹

In Ohio, resistance to the Church and to the Prophet Joseph Smith increased as the Church's economic position decreased and the Kirtland Safety Society inched toward failure. Inside the Church, apostasy spread. Outside the Church, hatred increased. In August 1837, apostates Warren Parrish (a former scribe to Joseph Smith) and John Boynton (a member of the Quorum of the Twelve) led a group armed with pistols and bowie knives and stormed the temple. Peace was restored, but by the fall of that year another group led by Parrish, Boynton, and Luke Johnson sought to overthrow the Church and take over the temple. Between November 1837 and June 1838 ten to fifteen percent of the Church's membership in Kirtland apostatized. In January 1838, Joseph Smith was warned of an assassination plot and had to be secreted out of town. War against the Saints in Ohio continued to escalate.

Again, the answer to rising conflict against the Prophet and the faithful Saints was not retaliation but withdrawal to the West. By 1838, Church leadership and Church headquarters were concentrated in northern Missouri. Tragically, opposition to the Church in Missouri would prove to be more intense and bitter than in New York or Ohio. It challenged the Saints' adherence to the Lord's requested response to conflict.

While the Saints were in Ohio, this other center of gathering had developed in Missouri. In 1831, the Prophet Joseph Smith had revealed that Independence, Jackson County, Missouri, was the center place of Zion, site of the future temple, and consecrated gathering place of the Saints, and that land should be purchased there (see D&C 57). By 1833, twelve hundred Saints had migrated to Jackson County, but mob violence was determined to drive them out. "Efforts to defend their rights through peaceful means only in-

C. C. A. Christensen (1831–1912), *Haun's Mill*, ca. 1865, tempera on muslin, 78 x 114 inches. Courtesy of Brigham Young University Museum of Art. All rights reserved.

furiated the Missourians further. . . . The Mormons' weak attempts at defense proved useless, and by the middle of November [1833] the Jackson County Saints were no more."[20] The exiles made their way across the Missouri River to the north in Clay County.

It was in the midst of these Missouri persecutions, in August of 1833, that Doctrine and Covenants 98 was revealed. It is instructive that as the intensity of the opposition increased, justifiably inclining the Saints toward revenge and retaliation, the Lord revealed His ancient law of warfare, discussed above, a law grounded in the principle of waiting patiently on the Lord. In February 1834, after the November expulsion of the Saints from Jackson County, the Lord called upon the Prophet to lead an expedition of Saints known as Zion's Camp to help restore the Missouri Saints' property and to protect them from further depredations. But in so doing, the Lord

"Renounce War and Proclaim Peace": Early Beginnings ★ 25

seems to have provided an addendum to the principles of war and retaliation given in section 98.

> Verily I say unto you, my friends, behold, I will give unto you a revelation and commandment, that you may know how to act in the discharge of your duties concerning the salvation and redemption of your brethren, who have been scattered on the land of Zion;
>
> Being driven and smitten by the hands of mine enemies, on whom I will pour out my wrath without measure in mine own time.
>
> For I have suffered them thus far, that they might fill up the measure of their iniquities, that their cup might be full;
>
> And that those who call themselves after my name might be chastened for a little season with a sore and grievous chastisement, because they did not hearken altogether unto the precepts and commandments which I gave unto them.
>
> But verily I say unto you, that I have decreed a decree which my people shall realize, inasmuch as they hearken from this very hour unto the counsel which I, the Lord their God, shall give unto them.
>
> Behold they shall, for I have decreed it, begin to prevail against mine enemies from this very hour. (D&C 103:1–6)

This revelation also spoke of the redemption of Zion by "power" (D&C 103:15). Though some Saints may have thought this implied conquest by force, the Prophet's intentions did not include military-style aggression, as further events surrounding Zion's Camp attest. While encamped on Fishing River, Missouri, Joseph received another revelation. It came as "mob violence against the saints in Missouri had increased, and organized bodies from several counties had declared their intent to destroy the people."[21] Yet, stunningly, the Lord concluded this revelation with a powerful command: "And again I say unto you, sue for peace, not only to the people that have smitten you, but also to all people; and lift up an ensign of peace, and make a proclamation of peace unto the ends of the earth; and make proposals for peace unto those who have smitten you, according to the voice of the Spirit which is in you, and all things shall work together for your good. Therefore, be faithful; and behold, and lo, I am with you even unto the end. Even so. Amen" (D&C 105:38–41). Zion's Camp disbanded without taking military action.

By the summer of 1838, the continuing and unresolved depredations against the Missouri Saints weighed heavily upon Church leaders. These concerns and frustrations seem to have boiled over in sermons delivered by Sidney Rigdon that season. His July 4 oration, held at the public square of Far West, Missouri, proved to be a pivotal moment in Mormon relations with neighboring Missourians. Elder Rigdon started out nobly enough, recounting the principles of freedom established by the founders of America. But he ended up announcing that the Saints were through suffering abuse from their enemies. "We have proved the world with kindness, we have suffered their abuse without cause, with patience, and have endured without resentment, until this day. . . . But from this day and this hour, we will suffer it no more. . . . That mob that comes on us to disturb us; it shall be between us and them a war of extermination, for we will follow them, till the last drop of their blood is spilled, or else they will have to exterminate us; for we will carry the seat of war to their own houses, and their own families, and one party or the other shall be utterly destroyed."[22]

Looking back six years later, Jedediah M. Grant said the speech "was the main auxiliary that fanned into a flame the burning wrath of the mobocratic portion of the Missourians. They now had an excuse, their former threats were renewed, and soon executed, [and] we were then . . . all made accountable for the acts of one man."[23]

President Brigham Young also placed blame for the Church's subsequent troubles on Rigdon's speech. "Elder Rigdon was the prime cause of our troubles in Missouri, by his fourth of July oration."[24]

Between August 6, 1838, and October 27, 1838, at least six significant conflicts broke out between the Mormons and the Missourians. The die was cast. On October 27, 1838, Governor Lilburn W. Boggs issued his infamous Extermination Order against the Mormons, they "having made war upon the people of this state."[25] The Lord's counsel had not been followed by everyone, and given all that He had said about renouncing war and continually holding up the standard of peace, it was with supreme irony that the Mormons were ordered to be "exterminated or driven from the State . . . for the *public peace.*"[26]

Again the Saints, guided by prophetic example, moved away from what could have been turned into massive armed conflict. They established a new city on the Mississippi at a place formerly called Commerce, Illinois, and thus created a new capital of their kingdom—Nauvoo. Once there, the Prophet Joseph did not abandon the Lord's principles of defensive war when divinely sanctioned. But he seemed to come to believe that such principles can profitably flow from a position of military as well as spiritual strength. Hence, the Nauvoo Legion was created in February 1841 as part of the charter granted to the city of Nauvoo. The legion was organized with two cohorts—the horse troops and the foot troops. Joseph Smith was elected commander of the legion with the rank of lieutenant general and John C. Bennett as second in command with the rank of major general.

Though the legion was "demonized by its critics as a symbol of Mormon militarism and empire-building," it was "defended by its supporters as a means of self defense."[27] Certainly the idea of the legion was a product of all that the Saints had suffered at the hands of their enemies. "From their 1833 expulsion from Independence to

C. C. A. Christensen (1831–1912), *Joseph Mustering the Nauvoo Legion*, ca. 1865, tempera on muslin, 78 x 114 inches. Courtesy of Brigham Young University Museum of Art. All rights reserved.

the slaughter at Haun's Mill in 1838, the Mormon stay in Missouri is written in blood. . . . Little wonder, then, that as they reassembled in Illinois self-defense was an uppermost priority."[28] But there was another factor in its establishment as well. The Nauvoo Legion was also a unit of the Illinois state militia, and service in the legion satisfied the Military Act of 1792, which required every able-bodied white male between the ages of eighteen and forty-five to enlist in their local militia. Thus, as Joseph Smith stated, the legion was not to be a Mormon-only organization, and the Prophet couched its existence in terms of self-defense for all citizens. He said, "The Legion is . . . a body of citizen soldiers organized . . . for the public defense, the general good, and the preservation of law and order—to save the innocent, unoffending citizens from the iron grasp of the oppressor, and perpetuate and sustain our free institutions against misrule, anarchy, and mob violence."[29]

The legion participated in parades, practice drills, mock battles, and other special occasions. But its very existence was foreboding to the naysayers and opponents of the Church. Even though the legion "was the product of a defensive rather than an aggressive psychology,"[30] it gave enemies of the Church an opportunity to vent their feelings and plant questions in the minds of already nervous non-Mormon citizens of the region. For example, Thomas Sharp, editor of the *Warsaw Signal*, wrote: "Why these weekly parades? Why all this strictness of discipline? We pause for reply. How military these people are becoming! Everything they say or do seems to breathe the spirit of military tactics. Their prophet appears, on all great occasions, in his splendid regimental dress, signs his name Lieutenant General, and more titles are to be found in the Nauvoo Legion than any one book on military tactics can produce. . . . Truly fighting must be part of the creed of these saints. Are the Danites still separate or merged with the Nauvoo Legion?"[31]

In truth, the Nauvoo Legion never engaged an enemy force or fired a shot in anger, but its presence helped to polarize fear and opposition toward the Mormons once more. As early as 1842, Governor Thomas Ford called for at least a modification of both the Nauvoo City Charter and the Nauvoo Legion. In June 1844, the Prophet was murdered, and the Nauvoo Legion was called out to guard the city from attack. In January 1845, Illinois revoked the Nauvoo Charter, and the legion ceased to exist legally. However, some of its members still felt it was needed to protect homes and property, and some of these legionnaires fought futilely in the Battle of Nauvoo in 1846 to prevent the fall of the city. By then, however, most of the Saints had left for the West. It was a pointless effort. President Brigham Young did ask remnants of the legion to help form militia units to protect the exiles during the Mormon exodus in 1846 and 1847. Some members of the legion later served in the Mormon Battalion.

Conclusion

The Nauvoo experience, like the experiences in New York, Ohio, and Missouri, tested the patience and resolve of the Saints to renounce war and proclaim peace. But many of them remained true to the revelations of God given through the Prophet Joseph Smith. The Saints learned by bitter experience that the history of opposition to the Church and to the Saints is one of constant, unrelenting persecution. It is a history of Satan's hand in the affairs of his fallen, temporary, mortal kingdom. However, it is also a history of the Lord's hand in the affairs of His eternal kingdom on earth.

War had a profound effect on the Saints in New York, Ohio, Missouri, and Illinois in the early part of this dispensation. It taught them that armed conflict causes misery and destruction. It made them keenly aware of the unfairness of mortality. It caused many to turn from the Church but caused others to turn to the Lord because He was their *only* recourse. Disagreeable as it was, war was a catalyst for the development of faith and for some of the most powerful revelations we know.

Through those revelations, the Lord has helped His disciples to understand the nature of war and what principles He, with His infinite knowledge, wisdom, and power, wants followed. War began in heaven with the rebellion of Lucifer against righteousness and agency, and it has continued to this very day. War is the result of greed, lust, and selfishness. The righteous are often drawn into war because of the need to defend home, family, land, country, liberty, and religion from the encroachment of an aggressor. The Lord has promised to fight the battles of the righteous against their aggressors, but if the Lord's people sin they will not have the Lord's protection.

The Lord's people must not be guilty of the first, second, or third offense. The Lord sometimes allows the righteous to be slain so that the wicked may be condemned and the righteous be given the blessings of heaven. Having to face armed conflict, depredation, and persecution impressed upon the Prophet Joseph Smith and his loyal supporters the kind of being God actually is.

The Prince of Peace wants peace! He wants His disciples to hold up the standard of peace in the face of war, even if it means withdrawing from a region for a time. Perhaps that is the greatest legacy left to us by the New York, Ohio, Missouri, and Illinois Saints. Their sacrifices and their responses to conflict show that it is possible to live as the Lord bids us—renounce war and proclaim peace and seek instead to turn the hearts of the children and the fathers to one another. They avoided conflict at great cost to themselves and their families, leaving their homes in the dead of winter, and sometimes sacrificing all of their material possessions. Unfortunately, these are lessons that come hard to those not so willing to follow the Lord's requests at all hazards—the proud, the impatient, the self-centered, and the short-sighted—in other words, those focused only on mortality. But obedience to the Lord's will in this matter brings nothing less than the approbation of heaven and the blessings of a godlike personality.

Notes

1. Thomas S. Monson, "Mercy—The Divine Gift," *Ensign*, May 1995, 54.

2. Gordon B. Hinckley, "The Times in Which We Live," *Ensign*, November 2001, 74.

3. Gordon B. Hinckley, "War and Peace," *Ensign*, May 2003, 78; emphasis added.

4. Heading to Doctrine and Covenants 98.

5. Spencer W. Kimball, "The False Gods We Worship," *Ensign*, June 1976, 3.

6. David O. McKay, in Conference Report, April 1942, 74.

7. Hinckley, "War and Peace," 80.

8. Llewelyn R. McKay, comp., *Secrets of a Happy Life: From the Writings and Discourses of David O. McKay* (Salt Lake City: Bookcraft, 1968), 76–77; emphasis in original.

9. Kimball, "False Gods," 3.

10. Daniel K Judd and Benjamin M. Rogers, "'Wars and Rumors of Wars': A Restoration Perspective," *Religious Educator* 5, no. 1 (2004), 103.

11. Ezra Taft Benson, "A World Message," *Improvement Era*, June 1970, 96.

12. See Mark E. Petersen, *The Great Prologue* (Salt Lake City: Deseret Book, 1975), 51–52.

13. Petersen, *The Great Prologue*, 57, quoting Wilson's History of the United States.

14. William H. Wilbur, *The Making of George Washington* (New York: Patriot Education, 1973), 198.

15. Joseph F. Smith, *Gospel Doctrine* (Salt Lake City: Deseret Book, 1986), 409; emphasis in original.

16. Harold B. Lee, in Conference Report, April 1942, 95–96.

17. Harold B. Lee, in Conference Report, October 1942, 73.

18. Joseph F. Smith, Anthon H. Lund, and Charles W. Penrose, in James R. Clark, ed., *Messages of the First Presidency* (Salt Lake City: Bookcraft, 1970), 4:325–26.

19. "Elder Kimball's Journal," *Times and Seasons*, January 15, 1845, 771.

20. Andrew H. Hedges, "Mobocracy in Jackson County," in *Joseph: Exploring the Life and Ministry of the Prophet*, ed. Susan Easton Black and Andrew C. Skinner (Salt Lake City: Deseret Book, 2005), 207. See the entire chapter for a succinct overview of the period 1831–33.

21. Heading to Doctrine and Covenants 105.

22. Quoted in Alexander L. Baugh, "'The Mormons Must Be Treated As Enemies,'" in *Joseph*, 289.

23. Quoted in Baugh, "Enemies," 289.

24. Quoted in Baugh, "Enemies," 289.

25. Quoted in Baugh, "Enemies," 292.

26. Quoted in Baugh, "Enemies," 284; emphasis added.

27. Richard E. Bennett, "The Nauvoo Legion," in *Joseph*, 358.

28. Bennett, "Nauvoo Legion," 359.

29. Quoted in Bennett, "Nauvoo Legion," 359.

30. Robert B. Flanders, *Nauvoo: Kingdom on the Mississippi* (Urbana: University of Illinois Press, 1965), 101.

31. Quoted in Bennett, "Nauvoo Legion," 393.

Introduction to the Mexican-American War

"I BELIEVE IT TO BE A WAR OF PRETEXTS, A WAR IN WHICH THE TRUE MOTIVE *is not distinctly avowed, but in which pretenses, afterthoughts, evasions and other methods are employed to put a case before the community which is not the true case."*
—*Daniel Webster, September 1847*

✷ ✷ ✷

INTERPRETATIONS CONCERNING THE CAUSES of the Mexican-American War vary. Simply stated, a dictatorial Centralist government in Mexico began the war in response to the United States' annexation of Texas, land that Mexico continued to claim despite the establishment of the independent Republic of Texas ten years before. Despite the many interpretations of its causes, the war resulted in new boundaries and new territories that reshaped the United States and Mexico forever.

At the onset of the war, Mexico had an unstable government. In December 1844, a coalition of moderates and

Federalists forced the dictator Antonio López de Santa Anna into exile and elected José Joaquín Herrera as acting president of Mexico. The Federalist victory was short and peace was uneasy. Although Santa Anna was exiled to Cuba, other Centralists began planning the overthrow of Herrera. With Mexico's internal strife, the annexation of Texas in 1845 fueled the conflict. The principal factor leading to the annexation of Texas was Britain's interest in an independent Texas.

Rather than resorting to an immediate declaration of war, as had been the promise of his predecessor, Herrera hoped for a negotiated settlement to the conflict. Then, fearing American patience was running short in negotiations over Texas, Herrera determined to settle the issue. He requested that the United States send an envoy to Mexico; President James K. Polk appointed John Slidell. Slidell was authorized to purchase California and New Mexico from Mexico and to settle the Texas boundary. While the Republic of Texas had claimed the Rio Grande as its boundary, the adjacent Mexican state of Tamaulipas claimed the area north of the Rio Grande to the Nueces River as the boundary.

By the time Slidell arrived in Mexico in December 1845, it was too late. The Herrera government was under intense fire from the Centralists. Herrera refused to meet with Slidell, and a few days later Centralist leader Mariano Parades y Arrillaga issued a revolutionary manifesto and entered Mexico City at the head of an army. Herrera fled and Parades assumed the presidency. After Slidell's failure, Polk ordered Zachary Taylor to move his army to the mouth of the Rio Grande and to prepare to defend Texas from invasion.

For the Centralists in Mexico, the annexation of Texas had been sufficient cause for war; they saw no disputed boundary—Mexico owned all of Texas. Before Taylor had moved to the Rio Grande, Parades had begun mobilizing troops. On April 23, Mexico declared war on the United States. On April 25, Mexican troops crossed the Rio Grande and ambushed a detachment of American dragoons commanded by Captain Seth B. Thornton. On May 11, Polk presented his war message to Congress, and two days later, despite abolitionist opposition, the U.S. Congress declared war on Mexico.

Mexican leaders had expected a relatively easy victory over the United States. Parades had spoken grandly of occupying New Orleans and Mobile. His army was four to six times the size of the U.S. army. Also, Mexican troops were well armed, disciplined, and, above all, experienced in revolutions.

At that time, American strength at the Rio Grande had risen to nearly twenty thousand troops, the majority of which were volunteers. Despite the troop mass, Americans were susceptible to subtropical diseases and struggled to maintain sanitary conditions in camps. Dysentery, fevers, and general debility spread through the camps. The mortality rate from sickness was staggering.

> **Mexican leaders had expected a relatively easy victory over the United States.**

As the war continued, the Centralist government became weaker until it collapsed. Rather than unite Mexico, the war had given the Federalist faction an opportunity to rebel. Taylor had been in contact with the Federalist faction in the fall of 1845. The Federalist leaders asked for assistance in ousting Parades and promised the Americans supplies in return.

In July 1846, Parades went into hiding, leaving his vice president in command. Soon after, the Centralists' government fell apart completely upon the resignation of the vice president, and the Federalists restored the constitution of 1824. In the meantime, Santa Anna had returned to Mexico, where he was appointed head of the Mexican army and in December was elected president by the

Mexican Congress. While Santa Anna gained control of the Mexican army, Taylor began his advance on Monterrey. After bloody fighting at Monterrey, the Mexican general Pedro de Ampudia requested a truce. On September 25, he was permitted to withdraw his forces from the city, and an eight-week armistice began.

In January 1847, Santa Anna traveled north with about twenty thousand men to repel Zachary Taylor's troops. Word of Santa Anna's approach reached Taylor on February 21. Although outnumbered almost three to one, Taylor took up a position at the hacienda of Buena Vista, a few miles from Saltillo. The Mexican troops forced the Americans to abandon important defensive positions and nearly overcame the U.S. troops. However, a salient charge led by Colonel Jefferson Davis and a resolute artillery advance under Captain Braxton Bragg saved the day for the Americans. Santa Anna withdrew that night and moved south to intercept Scott's invasion force. The American advance from Veracruz to Mexico City was the decisive campaign of the war. It began with an army of approximately twelve thousand, which was transported by sea to a beach about three miles south of Veracruz. Scott had successfully surrounded the city by March 15 and launched a combined naval and land attack on March 22. Heavy shelling from navy guns forced the almost impenetrable town to surrender six days later.

Almost immediately after the surrender, the Americans began to advance toward Mexico City. Only sporadic resistance was encountered until his army reached the village of Cerro Gordo, where Santa Anna had prepared to make the Americans retreat. The attack on Cerro Gordo was led by units under William J. Worth, Robert E. Lee, George B. McClellan, and Joseph E. Johnston. P. G. T. Beauregard helped find a trail that enabled the Americans to envelop and rout Santa Anna's forces, thus winning the battle for the United States.

During June and July, Santa Anna anxiously prepared to defend Mexico City. On August 7, the Americans began their advance from

Puebla. The first heavy fighting occurred at Contreras, just outside Mexico City. Santa Anna fell back to Churubusco, where he took up a defensive position in a convent. The Americans followed and soon forced them to surrender. However, Santa Anna and much of his command escaped. After an unsuccessful last effort to defend the city, Santa Anna evacuated his troops and the war was over. Sadly, Mexican War veterans continued to suffer from the debilitating diseases contracted during the campaigns, and many died soon after the conflict.

2

The Church and the Mexican-American War

LARRY C. PORTER

★ ★ ★

ON MAY 13, 1846, JUST MONTHS AFTER the first wagons began their westward exodus from Nauvoo, Illinois, the United States declared war on Mexico. In the emergency, President James K. Polk directed William L. Marcy, secretary of war, to prepare the necessary orders for the formation of a battalion of Iowa volunteers from among the camps of the Mormons, who were then on the plains of that territory. Accordingly, Marcy drew up instructions for Colonel

Larry C. Porter is a professor emeritus of Church history and doctrine at Brigham Young University.

Brigham Young, circa 1846. © by Intellectual Reserve, Inc.

Stephen W. Kearny on June 3, 1846, and sent them by dispatch to Fort Leavenworth, Kansas.[1]

Colonel Kearny, in turn, issued an order pertaining to Mormon enlistment to one of his experienced company commanders, Captain James Allen (later promoted to lieutenant colonel) of the First Dragoons. Accompanied by three men, Captain Allen made his first contact with the Mormons at Mount Pisgah, Iowa, and there read to the high council a circular he had issued explaining his mission.[2] Elder Wilford Woodruff, who was in the camp, sent a special messenger to alert President Brigham Young concerning the nature of Allen's request. And, after giving Allen a letter of introduction to William Clayton, clerk of the Camp of Israel, Elder Woodruff directed him to the principal encampment of the Saints at Council Bluffs.³

After he arrived at Council Bluffs, Captain Allen was invited to a meeting with President Young and his council, held on July 1, 1846, at the camp of John Taylor on Mosquito Creek. In addition to President Young, those in attendance were Heber C. Kimball, Willard Richards, Orson Hyde, Orson Pratt, George A. Smith, John Taylor, "Uncle" John Smith, Levi Richards, and others.⁴ Captain Allen made known the terms offered by the government, which were acceptable in principle to the council. An invitation was sent to the brethren of the camp to assemble. Captain Allen explained his orders from Colonel Kearny. President Young then commented on the proposal that a battalion be formed:

> I said, the question might be asked, Is it prudent for us to enlist to defend our country? If we answer in the affirmative, all are ready to go.
>
> Suppose we were admitted into the Union as a State, and the government did not call on us, we

Fort Leavenworth, Kansas

Built in 1827 by Colonel Henry Leavenworth and the Third Infantry Regiment, Fort Leavenworth served as a key military installation during the United States' westward expansion of the nineteenth century. During the Mexican-American War, Fort Leavenworth served as a staging area as well as supplier and outfitter of the Army of the West. During its early years, soldiers garrisoned at Fort Leavenworth were responsible for protecting supply trains heading west on the Santa Fe and Oregon trails. During the Civil War, Fort Leavenworth was the reception and training center for Kansas volunteers. After the war, the fort was assigned to provide protection to migrants and to oversee control of Native Americans on the Western Plains. In 1881, General William T. Sherman organized and established the School of Application for Cavalry and Infantry (now known as the U.S. Army Command and General Staff College) at Fort Leavenworth. This school soon became renowned for producing effective leaders and great military minds. Today, Fort Leavenworth stands as the oldest operating U.S. Army post west of the Mississippi River. It has never been subject to an enemy attack. Besides housing the Command and General Staff College, it is also home to the National Simulation Center and the U.S. Disciplinary Barracks (John W. Partin, ed., *A Brief History of Fort Leavenworth* [Fort Leavenworth, KS: Combined Arms Research Library, 1983]).

would feel ourselves neglected. Let the Mormons be the first to set their feet on the soil of California. Capt. Allen has assumed the responsibility of saying that we may locate at Grand Island, until we can prosecute our journey. This is the first offer we have ever had from the government to benefit us.

I proposed that the five hundred volunteers be mustered, and I would do my best to see all their families brought forward, as far as my influence extended, and feed them when I had anything to eat myself.[5]

The Mustering In

On July 16, 1846, Captain Allen summoned the four and a half companies of Iowa Mormon volunteers who had been recruited, and he formed the battalion into a hollow square at the designated location on Mosquito Creek.[6] Captain Allen mustered them into the service of the United States Army for the period of one year. The oath administered to enlistees during the Mexican War era reads as follows:

> I _____, do solemnly swear, that I will bear true allegiance to the United States of America, and that I will serve them honestly and faithfully against all their enemies or opposers whatsoever; and observe and obey the orders of the President of the United States, and the orders of the officers appointed over me, according to the Rules and Articles for the government of the armies of the United States.[7]

After the enlistment ceremony, James Allen was automatically designated a lieutenant colonel of infantry by order of Colonel Kearny at Fort Leavenworth, Kansas.

Elder Woodruff witnessed the formation of the companies by their captains and the mustering-in ceremony with the administration of its attendant oath and affirmation on that historic day, July 16, 1846.

The Saints enlist in the Mormon Battalion at Council Bluffs, Iowa, under the watchful eye of Captain James Allen and President Brigham Young. © by Intellectual Reserve, Inc.

James Allen (1806–46)

James Allen began his military career as a graduate of West Point. His graduating class of 1829 also included future Civil War general Robert E. Lee. Allen's first assignment found him at the edge of the wilderness in the Michigan Territory. He is credited with producing the first map correctly depicting the relationship between the many lakes and streams that form the Mississippi River. Later he was transferred to Fort Leavenworth, having been promoted to first lieutenant and attached to the First Regiment of Dragoons, where he served as an engineer in the exploration of the Indian territories of the southwest.

Captain James Allen.
Courtesy of Church Archives.

Not long after his transfer to Fort Leavenworth, Allen was promoted to captain and given command of Company I, First Regiment of Dragoons. His continued exploration of the area around the Des Moines River led to the founding of Fort Des Moines, later to become the city of Des Moines, Iowa.

It was perhaps his intimate knowledge of this area, gained by years of exploration, that led to receiving orders from Colonel Kearny of Fort Leavenworth to travel to Council Bluffs, Iowa, and organize five hundred Mormon soldiers for the war with Mexico. Having secured the volunteer force of Latter-day Saints, Captain Allen was promoted to lieutenant colonel and took command of the Mormon Battalion. Allen was immediately popular with the soldiers, but unfortunately his command lasted approximately one month, as he became ill and was forced to remain at Fort Leavenworth while he ordered his men to begin their march to California along the Santa Fe Trail. Soon afterward, he died of "congestive fever" on August 23, 1846, and became the first officer buried in what would later be named the Fort Leavenworth National Military Cemetery (Arnold K. Garr, Donald Q. Cannon, and Richard O. Cowan, eds., *Encyclopedia of Latter-day Saint History* [Salt Lake City: Deseret Book, 2000], 19).

The significance and nature of the enlistment of the battalion of Iowa Mormon Volunteers created very poignant feelings in his bosom. He wrote:

> When this 500 men were Called for they steped forth instantly at the Call of the President notwithstanding the Ill treatment & suffering we had endured in the Persecutions of the United States. Yes we steped forward as A People while in the midst of a long journey And left families teams wagons & cattle standing by the way side not expecting to meet with them again for one or two years. Yes wives & Children were left in this way to the mercy of God And the brethren And went away with Cheerful hearts Believing that they were doing the will of God. And while casting my eyes upon them I considered I was viewing the first Battalion of the Army of Israel engaged in the United States service for one year And going to lay the foundation of A far greater work even preparing the way for the building of Zion.[8]

That same day, Colonel Allen marched the command about eight miles south of Council Bluffs to Trader's Point, or Point aux Poules (on or near the Pottawattamie and Mills County line), on the Missouri River. Here, Peter A. Sarpy, a licensed government merchant, was authorized to issue provisions on credit to the U.S. Army. Members of the battalion were thus enabled to obtain blankets and other standard items needed to sustain them on their march to Fort Leavenworth, where they would finish being fitted out. The costs of their purchases were to be deducted from their first pay from the government.[9]

In addition to the approximately 503 men who were mustered in at Council Bluffs and the seven men who subsequently enlisted at Fort Leavenworth and Council Grove, Kansas, the U.S. Army made provision for each company to have four laundresses, for a total of twenty women in the battalion. Twelve young men under enlistment age were also designated as "servants of officers," and a few

Mormon Battalion Officers and the Civil War

Several of the officers in command of the Mormon Battalion served as military leaders during the American Civil War and later as civic leaders. At least three—Lieutenant Colonel Philip St. George Cooke, Lieutenant Andrew Jackson Smith, and Lieutenant George Stoneman—went on to play prominent roles as general officers during the Civil War. In addition, Stoneman later served as a political leader.

Though greatly disliked by the men of the Mormon Battalion for his strict and often harsh discipline, Andrew Jackson Smith later proved his ability as a military leader. At the outbreak of the Civil War, he was promoted to the rank of colonel and joined the Second California Volunteer Cavalry. By 1862 he had been given the rank of brigadier general in the U.S. Volunteers and was involved in many successful campaigns during the war, his most notable being a complete rout of General Nathan Bedford Forrest during the Battle of Tupelo in Mississippi.

George Stoneman was assigned to the First Dragoons out of West Point and then detailed as acting assistant quartermaster to the Mormon Battalion in their march to California. His service during the Civil War began early, while he was in command of Fort Brown, Texas. At the beginning of hostilities between the North and the South, Stoneman refused to relinquish the fort to Confederate authorities in the area. He was able to escape north with the majority of his command and soon joined the First U.S. Cavalry. He was selected adjutant to General George B. McClellan. His service as Cavalry Corps commander of the Army of the Potomac was largely unsuccessful because of that command's poor use of cavalry. Serving as scapegoat for the army's failures during several campaigns, Stoneman was relieved of his command and sent to Washington to serve in more administrative duties. Becoming quickly

Lt. George Stoneman   Lt. Andrew Jackson Smith

impatient with the tediousness of administration, Stoneman appealed to his home state of Ohio and was quickly reassigned as commander of the Cavalry Corps for the Army of Ohio, which fought in the Atlantic Campaign under General William Tecumseh Sherman.

In this new theater, Stoneman quickly found success participating in many successful battles and raids. In 1865 he almost captured Jefferson Davis, Confederate president. Stoneman retired from military service in 1871 and moved his family to California, where he settled in the San Gabriel Valley. He had fallen in love with California during his service there with the Mormon Battalion. He served as railroad commissioner for several years and then as governor of California from 1882 to 1886.

older men, such as Elisha Smith, acted as teamsters, driving private wagons. Allowances were also made for some wives and children to accompany their husbands and fathers, but the wives and children were required to provide their own transportation. Under this provision, thirty-five women, including the laundresses, and forty-two children, including the servants to officers, also marched. An older couple, John and Jane Boscoe, accompanied Captain Jefferson Hunt's family.

Beginning of the Long March

A steamboat, which was expected to transport the men down the Missouri River, never arrived at Trader's Point. Of necessity, Colonel Allen elected to follow the land route down the east side of the river through Iowa and Missouri and then cross over to Fort Leavenworth.[10] Four companies of the battalion commenced their march about noon on July 21. Company E moved downriver to meet them on July 22.

The first fatality occurred in the early morning hours of July 23. Between midnight and 1:00 a.m., Private Samuel Boley, of Company B, who had become ill soon after leaving Council Bluffs, died and "was wrapped in his blanket and buried in a rough lumber coffin, which was the best we could get."[11] Private Boley was but one of twenty-three men who died from a variety of causes during active duty—from first enlistment, July 16, 1846, to July 16, 1847—and also during the reenlistment period of Captain Daniel C. Davis's Company A, Mormon Volunteers, from July 21, 1847, to March 14, 1848. Other deaths also occurred among nonmilitary personnel associated with the battalion, and three members who had been mustered out of the service were killed by Indians during their return to the body of the Saints.[12]

After traveling about 160 miles on the east side of the Missouri River, the battalion was ferried across to the garrison at Fort

Leavenworth on August 1, 1846. Here they were issued tents, one tent to each mess of six men, and were directed to camp on the public square. They had marched the entire distance from Council Bluffs without the benefit of tents, lying on the open ground. One of the men commented, "Our tents, being new, and pitched in military order, presented a grand appearance, and the merry songs which resounded through the camp made all feel like 'casting dull care away.'"[13]

A number of new personnel were added to the battalion roster at Leavenworth, namely William Beddome, Thomas B. Finlay, Thomas Gilbert, and Robert W. Whitworth, who enlisted at that post. The battalion also received its equipage. Some of the men who had been designated as sharpshooters and hunters received new guns—cap-lock Yaugers. James S. Brown described some of the additional items of issue: "We got flintlock muskets, and accoutrements consisting of bayonets, cartridge-boxes, straps and belts, canteens, haversacks, etc., also a knapsack each. . . . With all the paraphernalia of soldiers, we seemed so burdened as to be able neither to run nor to fight."[14] When Colonel Allen observed the excitement of the men at the arsenal as they received their weapons, he quipped, "Stand back, boys; don't be in a hurry to get your muskets; you will want to throw the d—d things away before you get to California."[15]

Much-Needed Funds

Elders Parley P. Pratt, John Taylor, Orson Hyde, and Jesse C. Little met with the members of the battalion on August 4, 1846. These Brethren had come from Council Bluffs with the express purpose of collecting money for the families of the men and obtaining some assistance for the Church. Each battalion enlistee was given $42 outright, which represented his entire clothing allowance for the year ($3.50 per month). From this allotment, the men contributed $5,192 to the Brethren out of the approximately $21,000 paid them.[16] These monies proved of inestimable worth to the pioneer Saints in their movement to the Rocky Mountains. On August 20, 1846, President Brigham Young expressed the Saints' gratitude, from his camp at Cutler's Park, Nebraska, for this selfless service of the battalion: "We consider the money you have received, as compensation for your clothing, a peculiar manifestation of the kind of providence of our Heavenly Father at this particular time, which is just the time for the purchase of provisions and goods for the winter supply of the camp." That same day, the Church council at Cutler's Park authorized sending a man into Missouri with a thousand dollars to buy wheat for the Camp of Israel.[17] The effect of their generosity was immediate.

Captain Jefferson Hunt, senior Mormon officer in the battalion. Courtesy of Church Archives.

The men also donated funds to Elders Parley P. Pratt, Orson Hyde, and John Taylor to help them on their missions to England. Similarly, assistance was given Elder Jesse C. Little on his return to the Eastern States Mission.[18] Some of the men outfitted themselves with new clothes and shoes to replace worn-out items for the march. Others chose to make do with what they had so they could conserve or send monies to their families.

On August 13, 1846, Companies A, B, and E began the march from Fort Leavenworth to Santa Fe via Bent's Fort.[19] Companies C and D were still not equipped to move out and so followed on August 15. Unfortunately, the battalion commander, Colonel Allen, became ill and remained at Leavenworth to recover. Colonel Allen turned the command over to Captain Jefferson Hunt, commander of Company A and the senior Mormon officer, directing him to set a course for Council Grove until he was able to rejoin the unit.

Levi Ward Hancock

A tremendous storm, bolstered by severe winds and heavy rains, swept the camp on August 20. As the turbulence finally passed, the men of the battalion could be heard giving thanks to the God of Israel for sparing their lives. Levi Hancock, one of the Seven Presidents of Seventy and the only General Authority on the march, requested that Captain Jefferson Hunt allow them to hold a religious meeting with the men to express thanksgiving. Samuel H. Rogers remembers that they also received "first-rate instructions" from Daniel Tyler, Levi W. Hancock, William Hyde, David Pettegrew (Pettigrew), and Captain Hunt, "concerning our duties as soldiers of the United States, as Saints, and particularly as Elders of Israel, as men who have received endowments in the Temple of the Lord, admonishing us to observe our Covenants, and to conduct ourselves in all our deportment as belonging to the family of heaven, as

One notable member of the battalion of volunteers was Elder Levi Ward Hancock, member of the Quorum of the Seventy and the only General Authority in the ranks of the Mormon Battalion.

Levi Ward Hancock. Courtesy of Church Archives.

Born in Massachusetts, Elder Hancock was very concerned with spiritual matters even from a young age and was nicknamed "Little Christian" by his siblings and friends. He had been taught by his mother that God hears and answers prayers, and as such "began to call upon the Lord seriously." At age twenty-seven, when Elder Parley P. Pratt and three other missionaries visited his hometown, Levi listened with great interest, saying, "I gathered faith and [i]t seemed like a wash of something warm took me in the face and ran over my body which gave me a feeling I cannot describe. The first word I said was 'it is the truth, I can feel it.'" He followed Elder Pratt back to Kirtland, Ohio, and was baptized and immediately ordained an elder and sent back to his hometown on a mission. Elder Hancock served several missions for the Church in Canada, the Northeast, and Missouri. He was also a member of Zion's Camp. A carpenter by trade, he helped build many of the buildings for the Saints settling Jackson County, including the Print Office, later destroyed by a mob. In 1835, Levi Ward Hancock was chosen as a member of the first Quorum of Seventy and was called to serve as one of the seven Presidents of Seventy. He served faithfully as a General Authority for the rest of his life (courtesy of Keith Perkins).

sons of the Most High. We were also entreated to . . . prove ourselves good and loyal subjects of the government of the United States, notwithstanding we had been persecuted by its citizens."[20]

Colonel Allen Replaced

On August 26, Second Lieutenant Samuel L. Gully and Sergeant Sebert C. Shelton brought sad news to the camp that Colonel Allen had died of "congestive fever" at Fort Leavenworth on August 23. Sergeant William Hyde expressed the sentiments of the command when he recorded: "This information struck a damper to our feelings as we considered him a worthy man, and from the kind treatment which the battalion had received from him, we had begun to look upon him as our friend, and a person from whom we should receive kind treatment."[21] Colonel Allen was buried fifth man in on "Officer Row A" at the post cemetery.

Lieutenant Colonel Clifton Wharton, then commanding officer at Fort Leavenworth, dispatched First Lieutenant Andrew Jackson Smith, of the First Dragoons, to Council Point, where he met with the officers of the battalion. Captain Jefferson Hunt had retained command of the troops to this point. However, Lieutenant Smith, a West Point graduate, explained his ability as a regular army officer to sign for quartermaster stores and conduct official correspondence, while they had not received their commissions or their certificates of command. With assurances that Colonel Allen's promises to the battalion would be carried out, the officers voted that Smith assume command. He then became the acting lieutenant colonel[22] of the battalion.

Dr. George B. Sanderson of Platte County, Missouri, who had received an appointment as assistant surgeon of volunteers at Fort Leavenworth on August 20, accompanied Lieutenant Smith. Dr. Sanderson was a contract surgeon hired by the U.S. Army. The men of the battalion soon developed a prejudice against him. The large doses of calomel he prescribed that he administered with an old "iron spoon" created considerable resentment. Dr. William L. McIntyre, a "good botanic physician" and a Latter-day Saint, was not allowed to administer any medicine to the men without Dr. Sanderson's orders. Hostilities developed between the men and Lieutenant A. J. Smith over his demands that the men report to Dr. Sanderson's wagon for sick call.[23]

With the arrival of Lieutenant Smith and Dr. Sanderson came a page of battalion history that needs to be completed. Sergeant Daniel Tyler mentions the presence of "negro servants" accompanying the two men.[24] Who these black bond servants were and how many there were is unknown. They go unnamed and yet were participants in the march who should be recognized.

The battalion reached the Arkansas River on September 11, 1846. The next day, while making their way up the river, they were surprised to meet a group of eight Latter-day Saints coming downstream. Their captain was William Crosby, and the company was on its way from Fort Pueblo, Colorado, to Monroe County, Mississippi, to bring out members of their families whom they had left behind. The "Mississippi Saints" from Monroe County, Mississippi, and Perry County, Illinois, were said by Crosby to number forty-three persons and nineteen wagons.[25] The company originally planned to join Brigham Young for an anticipated journey to the Great Salt Lake Valley during the 1846 season. However, they had missed their contact with President Young. The Mississippi Saints continued their journey to a point just a few miles east of Fort Laramie, on the Platte River. Here, they found that the main pioneer company under Brigham Young had not arrived and were not expected until the following year. They determined they must find a place to spend the winter. At that juncture, they met a French trapper named John Reshaw. He recommended that Fort Pueblo, Colorado, at the head

The Mormon Battalion fords the Arkansas River. Courtesy of Church Archives.

of the Arkansas River—a post for mountaineers, traders, and trappers—would serve their needs. Accepting his advice, Reshaw served as their guide to Fort Pueblo.[26]

Departure for Pueblo

The chance meeting of the Mormon Battalion with William Crosby on September 11 introduced an unexpected option to Lieutenant Smith that took shape as the battalion continued its march up the Arkansas River. Struggling to maintain the discipline of an arduous march, Lieutenant Smith felt very keenly the burden of so many families and saw that a growing number of men were becoming disabled because of illness. On September 15, 1846, the worsening condition of Private Alva Phelps of Company E undoubtedly influenced Lieutenant Smith's command to send certain individuals and families that were obviously struggling with health and the difficulties of the march to recoup at the Mormon encampment at Fort Pueblo. Private Phelps died on the evening of September 16.[27] Lieutenant Smith detailed Captain Nelson Higgins and a small contingent of soldiers to escort selected families to Pueblo. They left on the morning of September 16. This escort was to then rejoin the main unit in Santa Fe.[28] Although there were heated protests at the ordered separation, it would, in retrospect, provide a needed reprieve for some from the physical hardships created by an inhospitable environment. The Higgins Detachment, which separated from the main body on September 16 and arrived at Pueblo during October, consisted of fifty-five persons: thirteen men, nine women, and thirty-three children.[29]

The main body of the battalion then commenced a fifty-mile trek across the dreary Cimarron Desert, during which the marchers suffered extensively from the heat and lack of water. When water was periodically encountered, it was gratefully received. Sergeant Daniel Tyler declared: "We passed one lone pond full of insects of all sizes and shapes. Out of this pond we drove several thousand Buffalo. Even when the water was not roiled it was discolored and had a most disgusting appearance. The animals, doubtless, rendered it more noisome than it otherwise would have been by gathering in it to defend themselves from the flies. . . . The few whose canteens and flagons were not exhausted, of course did not use it, but, bad as it was, it was very welcome to most of us."[30]

Colonel Alexander W. Doniphan, friend and former legal counsel to the Church. Courtesy of Church Archives.

Arrival in Santa Fe

Having crossed what is now the state of Kansas, the southeast corner of Colorado, and the northwest tip of the Oklahoma Panhandle, the Mormon Battalion finally reached Santa Fe, New

Mexico, in two staggered elements. Lieutenant Smith, with an advanced unit of 250 men and a series of forced marchers, was the first contingent to arrive on October 9, 1846. They received a gun salute from the rooftops, as directed by their old friend and former legal counsel during the former trouble of the Saints in Missouri, Colonel Alexander W. Doniphan, commander of the garrison. The rear element of the Mormon Battalion, under command of First Lieutenant George Oman, with many who were ailing, marched in on October 12. One onlooker described the greeting exchanged between the Mormon and Mexican women on that occasion: "When the wagons containing the women stopped at the plaza, all the Mexican women near went up and shook hands with them, apparently both rejoiced and surprised to see them. The kindness and hospitality of the women throughout Mexico is proverbial, and in this instance the burst of feeling was as cordial and warm as a greeting of old friends and acquaintances after a long separation."[31]

Brigadier General Stephen W. Kearny, commander of the Army of the West, had been anxious to reach the center of his operations in California and had departed Santa Fe before the arrival of the battalion. On the Rio Grande he had received an express notifying him of the death of Colonel Allen. Kearny immediately issued orders on October 2, appointing Captain Philip St. George Cooke, then in the general's camp, to take command of the Mormon Battalion as acting lieutenant colonel.[32]

Colonel Brown's Sick Detachment

Returning to Santa Fe, Colonel Cooke restructured certain components of the battalion. Lieutenant Smith was to act as commissary of subsistence, and Brevet Second Lieutenant George Stoneman of the First Dragoons received the assignment as assistant quartermaster. Major Jeremiah H. Cloud acted as additional paymaster of volunteers. Captain James Brown was ordered to form a detachment of "the men reported by assistant Surgeon as incapable, from sickness and debility, of undertaking the present march to California." The detachment also included the four laundresses from each of the five companies. The detachment was to be transported to a place "near the source of the Arkansas river"—Fort Pueblo.[33]

The design was for all the women and children, except some servants of officers, to join the earlier Higgins detachment in Pueblo. However, a remonstration by some of the women and their spouses was amicably settled when two wives of officers and two wives of noncommissioned officers were allowed to continue the march with their husbands to California—that is, Lydia Edmunds Hunter, who would give birth to a son, Diego (James) Hunter, at San Diego, California, on April 20, 1847; Susan (Susanna) Moses Davis and

Philip St. George Cooke (1809–95)

A Virginia native, Philip St. George Cooke graduated from the U.S. Military Academy in 1827 as a second lieutenant and was sent to the West. Before his service in the Mexican-American War and as leader of the Mormon Battalion, Cooke fought in the Black Hawk War of 1832 under the command of General Henry Atkinson. His leadership and association with the Mormon Battalion led to a lasting friendship with the Church as well as a close, personal friendship with Brigham Young. Despite this, he was ordered to take part in the Utah Expedition under command of General Albert Sidney Johnston. After serving as an official U.S. military observer in the Crimean War, Colonel Cooke returned to Utah to take command of Camp Floyd until the outbreak of the Civil War forced his return to Washington.

Philip St. George Cooke. Courtesy of Church Archives.

After being promoted to brigadier general, Cooke led a brigade of regular army cavalry for a short time during General George B. McClellan's Peninsula Campaign, but then served in more administrative positions for the remainder of the war. Although a native of Virginia, Cooke chose to join the Union, a decision that fractured his family. Of three daughters and one son, only one of his daughters followed him to the Union side. She later married a Union general. Cooke's military career ended in 1873 with his retirement as a brevet major general after more than fifty years of service. He died in 1895 in Detroit, Michigan (Garr, Cannon, and Cowan, *Encyclopedia of Latter-day Saint History*, 245).

her four-year-old son, Daniel C. Davis Jr.; Phebe Draper Palmer Brown; and Melissa Burton Coray. When Sophia Tubbs, wife of Private William Tubbs, was denied her wish to go, she stowed away in a wagon and came out only when it appeared too late to send her back. However, William became so ill that he could not continue, and the Tubbses became part of the later Willis sick detachment to Pueblo from the Rio Grande. Of the women in the battalion, only the four named above reached their California destination.

Captain James Brown's detachment took up its march from Santa Fe to Pueblo on October 18, 1846, and the unit arrived at its destination on November 17. The contingent was made up of 128 individuals, including twenty women and nine children, one of whom, Fent F. Allred, was born en route to Pueblo from Santa Fe.[34]

Originally, a number of underage young men and some older men who were not enlisted in the battalion accompanied the unit from Council Bluffs as servants of officers. However, after the departure of the Higgins and Brown detachments, only the following individuals remained for the march from Santa Fe to California: Henry A. Bowing, who later enlisted in Captain Daniel Davis's reenlistment company, Company A, Mormon Volunteers in California[35]; Charles Edwin Colton, son of Private Philander Colton; Nathan Hart, son of Elias Hart; James A. Mowery, brother of Private John Thomas Mowery; William Byram Pace, son of First Lieutenant James Pace; Wilson Daniel Pace, son of William Franklin Pace; Zemira Palmer, son of Phebe Draper Palmer Brown by her first husband, George Palmer; Elisha Smith, who was hired by Captain Davis as a personal teamster and who died en route to California on December 5, 1846, near Ash Creek, New Mexico; and Nathan Young, son of Valentine W. Young.[36]

Colonel Cooke and the battalion departed Santa Fe on October 19. Their route took them to the Rio Grande and downriver to a point approximately where the small community of Williamsburg, New Mexico, is today. This is the site where General Kearny had left the river and had begun his more direct march toward the Gila River and on to California. He had taken pack animals, leaving the charge to Colonel Cooke to go farther south and prepare a wagon road to the Pacific.

Private James Hampton died at camp on the Rio Grande on November 3, 1846, and others were failing badly. Soon afterward, Colonel Cooke deemed it advisable to send a third detachment of sick personnel to Santa Fe for reassignment by the post commander, Colonel Sterling W. Price.[37] This detached command, under Second Lieutenant William W. Willis, commenced the excruciating journey

> Although it was contrary to orders, virtually every man had loaded his musket for protection.

on November 10, during the middle of winter. Levi Hancock painfully remembered the departure of his ailing brethren. He lamented: "Such a sight I never saw they was stowed away in the wagon like so many dead Hogs no better way could be done so it was said I went to the Lieu [Lieutenant Willis] and asked him if he would see that they was well taken care of when he had it in his power to do it and gave him my hand he griped it and I could say no more neather could he many gave me there hand."[38]

Sixty-two men, one woman, and one child comprised the march unit bound for Pueblo.[39] At Santa Fe, Colonel Price ordered the Willis detachment to proceed on to Pueblo for their winter quarters, where they arrived on December 20.[40] Colonel Cooke's reduced battalion now numbered 343 men. This figure included seven members of the command and staff and 336 company personnel.[41]

There were also ten additional men whose names we know who acted as guides and interpreters. They were variously hired by

The Church and the Mexican-American War

The Battle of the Bulls. Courtesy of Church Archives.

the military during the march sequence and were assigned to help pilot the battalion to California, namely Philip Thompson; Willard Preble Hall; Antoine Leroux; Pauline W. Weaver, whom General Kearny met on the Gila River (Arizona) when Weaver was coming out of California and sent him as a guide for Cooke; Jean Baptiste Charbonneau; Dr. Stephen Clark Foster, hired as an interpreter; Francisco, who had accompanied General Kearny and who was later sent back to assist Colonel Cooke; Appolonius; Chacon; and Tasson.[42]

Battle of the Bulls

Continuing the march, Colonel Cooke ordered his bugler to "blow to the right" near what is today Hatch, New Mexico, and the battalion headed west—away from the Rio Grande. Cutting through the southeast corner of present-day Arizona, the column moved into Old Mexico, reaching the ruins of the abandoned Rancho San Bernardino on December 2, 1846. Reentering Arizona, they marched along the San Pedro River, encountering hundreds of wild cattle that had congregated in the bottoms along the stream near present-day Charleston, Arizona. Battalion hunters with their Yaugers wounded two animals that stampeded into the column. Although it was contrary to orders, virtually every man had loaded his musket for protection. As more bulls approached the marchers, a battle followed. Sergeant Tyler reported:

> One small lead mule in a team was thrown on the horns of a bull over its mate on the near side, and the near mule, now on the off side and next to the bull, was gored. . . . One or two pack-mules were also killed. The end-gates of one or two wagons were stove in, and the sick, who were riding in them, were of course frightened. Some of the men climbed upon the wheels of the wagons and poured deadly fire into the enemy's ranks. Some threw themselves down and allowed the beasts to run over them; others fired and dodged behind mezquit brush to re-load their guns, while the beasts kept them dodging to keep out of the way. Others, still, climbed up in small trees, there being now and then one available.
>
> Brother Amos Cox was thrown about ten feet into the air, while a gore from three or four inches in length and about two or three in depth was cut in the inside of his thigh near its junction with the body. Sanderson sewed up the wound. Cox was an invalid for a long time, but finally recovered.[43]

Trouble near Tucson

Rather than following the San Pedro to its junction with the Gila River, Colonel Cooke elected to march overland to Tucson through a trackless waste with little water and a good deal of physical suffering. As they approached Tucson, battalion guides Antoine (Joaquin) Leroux, Pauline W. Weaver, Stephen C. Foster, Chacon, and Tasson reconnoitered the area and learned that about two hundred Mexicans had been gathered for the defense from several presidios of Sonora and that the garrison was commanded by Commandante Don Antonio Comaduran. Dr. Stephen Foster was captured by the Mexicans while scouting the enemy position. Concerned over Dr. Foster's long delay in returning, and not knowing whether he was being held, Colonel Cooke secured four Mexican soldiers as hostages. These soldiers had been encountered on the morning of December 15, 1846, and were taken prisoner. One of the Mexicans was reportedly the son of Commandante Comaduran. An exchange of hostages occurred between the two forces. Negotiations over the fate of Tucson broke down, and the Americans prepared for battle.

Comaduran's forces abandoned the community and withdrew to the nearby Mission of San Xavier del Bac. The battalion entered Tucson unopposed on December 16, 1846. Colonel Cooke instructed the soldiers to show respect to the people and their individual property rights. However, some public property, administered by the civil government and consisting of fifteen hundred bushels of wheat, was confiscated and issued to the hungry men and animals. Desiring to maintain Tucson as an established outpost of civilization against the marauding Apache Indians, the Mormon Battalion did nothing to destroy or impair the garrison. On December 18, the soldiers resumed their march northwest, leaving the presidio to Comaduran and its Mexican inhabitants.[44]

After traversing seventy miles of difficult desert terrain, the battalion finally reached the Gila and camped on the river bottoms just east of present-day Sacaton, Arizona. Here they enjoyed the hospitality of the Pima Indians. These cordial people brought corn, wheat, flour, pumpkins, and other refreshing foods to the famished

California Gold Rush of 1849

In 1848, John Sutter contracted with James Marshall to construct a sawmill on the south fork of the American River. Marshall, who had been Sutter's neighbor, had returned from his service in the Mexican-American War to find that he had lost his ranch and all of his cattle. The mill provided another possibility for an income. After scouting a suitable location for the mill, Marshall enlisted the help of members of the Mormon Battalion who had just been mustered out of the army and were on their way home to Salt Lake City. After completion of the mill, the workers discovered that the mill's tailrace did not provide enough water volume to operate the wood saws effectively. Marshall devised a plan to let the river's flow, with help, naturally carve out a greater tailrace. This had to be accomplished during the night so that the men weren't endangered while working in the mill during the day. It was Marshall's practice first thing each morning to inspect the work done during the nighttime.

On the morning of January 24, 1848, while inspecting the waterways below the mill, Marshall noticed several shiny particles in the water. Marshall reported:

> I picked up one or two pieces and examined them attentively; and having some general knowledge of minerals, I could not call to mind more than two which in any way resembled this—*sulphuret of iron,* very bright and brittle; and *gold,* bright, yet malleable. I then tried it between two rocks, and found that it could be beaten into a different shape, but not broken. I then collected four or five pieces and went up to Mr. Scott (who was working at the carpenters bench making the mill wheel) with the pieces in my hand and said, "I have found it." (quoted in "The Discovery of Gold in California," *Hutchings Illustrated California Magazine*, November 1857, 200–201)

Marshall was uncertain of the date but later settled on January 19, 1848. However, Mormon Battalion member Henry William Bigler kept a daily diary, which identifies the date as January 24, 1848, generally accepted by historians as correct.

News of this discovery quickly found its way into the newspapers of the eastern United States and before long throughout the world. Soon, prospectors by the thousands were converging on the American and Sacramento rivers in hopes of finding gold and securing their fortunes. While members of the Mormon Battalion were among the first to collect gold from the riverbed, virtually none stayed to earn their fortunes but collected only enough to fund their journey east toward Zion.

men.⁴⁵ The battalion next marched fifteen miles to the Maricopa Indian settlement, where they met three guides sent by General Kearny. These men were to direct them over the trail to Warner's Ranch, the first permanent settlement they would encounter in California. The soldiers camped at the Maricopa village that night. Sergeant Tyler described the Indian homes:

> They lived in dome-shaped houses, thatched with corn-stalks and straw, varying from about twenty to fifty feet in diameter, with arbors in front, on which lay, piled up, cotton stalks, with unopened bolls, to dry. This was probably from late crops, as the rule for picking out cotton is when the bolls open in the field. We saw domesticated animals here, the horse, mule, ox, dog and even Spanish fowls. Their implements of husbandry consisted of axes, hoes, shovels, and harrows. . . . The natives showed no signs of fear, and did not run like the Apaches, who, at the time, were said to be hostile.
>
> Colonel Cooke very kindly suggested to our senior officers that this vicinity would be a good place for the exiled Saints to locate. A proposition to this effect was favorably received by the Indians.⁴⁶

A limited examination of the Pima country was carried out with the colonel's blessing. In later years, numbers of battalion men, including members of the Pueblo, Colorado, detachment, established themselves in various parts of Arizona. Among them were Rufus C. Allen, Reuben Allred, Henry G. Boyle, Henry W. Brizzee, Edward Bunker, William A. Follett, Schyler Hulett, Hyrum Judd, Zadock K. Judd, Christopher Layton, William B. Maxwell, David Pulsipher, Samuel H. Rogers, Lot Smith, Henry Standage, George Steele, John Steele, and Samuel Thompson.⁴⁷

Desert March

After crossing the Colorado River near Yuma and entering a fifty-mile stretch of present-day Mexico, the battalion encountered the trials of the Imperial Desert. Veering northeast into California, the marchers negotiated the difficulties of Box Canyon and preserved the integrity of "Cooke's Wagon Road" against seemingly insurmountable odds. At Warner's Ranch, they were able to recoup sufficiently for a sustained march to the Pacific Ocean.

> "How Sweet and refreshing is the breeze that is winging its way from the ocean up this fertile valley."

Although Colonel Cooke's orders directed him to San Diego, he had assessed the military situation and determined to march to Los Angeles. However, a messenger from General Kearny met the battalion in the Temecula Valley on January 25 and redirected them to San Diego.[48] On January 27, the unit halted briefly at the deserted San Luis Rey Mission. For Samuel H. Rogers this was "the best building I have seen since entering Mexican territory."[49] Colonel Cooke described the mission:

> This is a fine large church of stuccoed brick, with an immense quadrangle of apartments with a corridor, and pillars and arches on each side within and on one face without. There are all the arrangements and appurtenances of a monastery, not omitting the wine apartments and brewery. I saw furniture and some paintings, but no occupants. The church was closed; it had a steeple with bells. In the center of the court is an oblique sundial, with orange and pepper trees, etc., in four large walled beds. The orange tree

The Mormon Battalion is officially mustered out of service in Los Angeles, July 16, 1847. Courtesy of Church Archives.

was bearing fruit of the size of a walnut. The Indians, too, had disappeared. Some two hundred of them I left in Temécula.[50]

Their first long-sought-after view of the Pacific was experienced from a bluff about a mile south of the mission. The emotions of Private Henry Boyle perhaps reflected those of his comrades as they surveyed the body of water they had journeyed so far to see:

> I never Shall be able to express my feelings at this enraptured moment. when our colums were halted evry eye was turned toward its placid Surface evry heart beat with muttered pleasure every Soul was full of thankfulness, evry tongue was Silend, we all felt too ful to give Shape to our feelings by any expression. . . . The Surrounding hills are covered with wild oats & grass nearly a foot high, green & luxuriant as midsummer and how Sweet and refreshing is the breeze that is winging its way from the ocean up this fertile valley which Stretches itself from the Shore back to the "Sieras". What an expansive view! how bright & beautiful evry thing looks!![51]

Arrival in San Diego

The battalion reached the Mission of San Diego a little before sunset on January 29, 1847. Colonel Cooke voiced his satisfaction with the accomplishments of the Mormon Battalion in a written order that, though dated January 30, 1847, was not read to the men until February 4.[52] Interestingly, when the order was read, the men were no longer at the San Diego Mission but rather back at the San Luis Rey Mission. On January 31, 1847, the battalion was ordered to return to San Luis Rey for garrison duty. The march from San Diego began February 1, 1847, and the troops arrived on the third. This was a strategic move that would give General Kearny some flexibility if there were hostilities at Los Angeles or San Diego. The entire battalion remained at San Luis Rey from February 3 to March 19, 1847.[53] Adjutant Philemon C. Merrill read the colonel's order on February 4, as follows:

Order Number 1
Headquarters Mormon Battalion
Mission of San Diego, January 30, 1847

The lieutenant-colonel commanding congratulates the battalion on their safe arrival on the shore of the Pacific ocean, and the conclusion of the *march of over two thousand miles*. History may be searched in vain for an equal march of infantry. Nine-tenths of it has been through a wilderness where nothing but savages and wild beasts are found, or deserts where, for want of water, there is no living creature. There, with almost hopeless labor, we have dug deep wells which the future traveler will enjoy. Without a guide who had traversed them, we have ventured into trackless prairies where water was not found for several marches. With crowbar and pick and ax in hand we have worked our way over mountains which seemed to defy aught save the wild goat, and hewed a passage through a chasm of living rock more narrow than our wagons.

To bring these first wagons to the Pacific, we have preserved the strength of our mules by herding them ever over large tracts, which you have laboriously guarded without loss. The garrisons of four *presidios* of Sonora, concentrated within the walls of Tucson, gave us no pause. We drove them out with their artillery, but our intercourse with the citizens was unmarked by a single act of injustice. Thus, marching half naked and half fed, and living upon wild animals, we have discovered and made a road of great value to our country. Arrived at the first settlement of California after a single day's rest, you cheerfully turned off from the route to this point of promised repose to enter upon a campaign, and meet, as we believed, the approach of the enemy; and this, too, without even salt to season your sole subsistence of fresh meat. Lieutenants A. J. Smith and George Stonemen, of the First dragoons, have shared and given valuable aid in all these labors. Thus, volunteers, you have exhibited some high and essential qualities of veterans. But much remains undone. Soon you will turn your strict attention to the drill, to system and order, to forms also, which are all necessary to the soldier.

By order of Lieutenant-colonel P. St. Geo. Cooke,
P. C. Merrill, Adjutant.[54]

Components of the Mormon Battalion continued to perform garrison duty and various detached service until the termination of their enlistment, when they were mustered out of the U.S. Army at Fort Moore, Los Angeles, on July 16, 1847.

The men of the Mormon Battalion had been called upon to enlist and to leave their families and friends in destitute circumstances. They did so knowing their enlistment would greatly aid the westward migration of the Saints, assist in the building of Zion, and render the requested patriotic service to their country during the emergency. On December 19, 1847, at the Log Tabernacle in Kanesville (Council Bluffs), Iowa, President Brigham Young, referring to the presence of some of the battalion boys who had returned to the Midwest following their term of enlistment, said to President Heber C. Kimball and others, "These men were the salvation of this Church."[55]

Notes

This chapter was modified from a chapter in David F. Boone and others, eds., *Regional Studies in Latter-day Saint Church History: California* (Provo, UT: Religious Studies Center, Brigham Young University, 1998), 31–56.

1. Philip St. George Cooke, "Cooke's Journal of the March of the Mormon Battalion, 1846–1847," in *Exploring Southwestern Trails, 1846–1854*, ed. Ralph P. Bieber and Averam B. Bender, vol. 7 of *The Southwest Historical Series* (Glendale, CA: Arthur H. Clark, 1938), 23.

2. Journal History of The Church of Jesus Christ of Latter-day Saints, June 26, 1846; Scott G. Kenney, ed., *Wilford Woodruff's Journal, 1833–1898* (Midvale, UT: Signature Books, 1983–84), 3:54–55.

3. Elden J. Watson, ed., *Manuscript History of Brigham Young, 1846–1847* (Salt Lake City: Elden J. Watson, 1971), 201–2.

4. Watson, *Manuscript History of Brigham Young*, 203–7.

5. Watson, *Manuscript History of Brigham Young*, 205–7. In this and all other quotations, original spelling and grammar have been retained.

6. Mosquito Creek is near the Iowa School for the Deaf at the junction of present U.S. Highway 275 and State Highway 92, on the southeast edge of Council Bluffs.

7. Letter of John J. Slonaker, Chief, Historical Reference Branch, U.S. Army Military History Institute, Carlisle Barracks, Carlisle, Pennsylvania, to Larry C. Porter, May 31, 1996.

8. Kenney, *Wilford Woodruff's Journal*, 3:60.

9. Erwin G. Gudde, ed., *Bigler's Chronicle of the West: The Conquest of California, Discovery of Gold, and Mormon Settlement as Reflected in Henry William Bigler's Diaries* (Berkley: University of California Press, 1992), 19.

10. John F. Yurtinus, "A Ram in the Thicket: The Mormon Battalion in the Mexican War," 2 vols. (PhD diss., Brigham Young University, 1975), 1:62–63.

11. Daniel Tyler, *A Concise History of the Mormon Battalion in the Mexican War, 1846–1847* (n.p.: Sergeant Daniel Tyler, 1881), 131.

12. Other deaths associated with the Mormon Battalion include Lt. Col. James Allen, Battalion Commander; Pvt. Marvin S. Blanchard, Company A; Pvt. Richard Carter, Company B; Pvt. Abner Chase, Company D; Pvt. George Coleman, Company A; Pvt. Eli Dodson, Company A; Pvt. Neal Donald, Company C; Pvt. Albert Dunham, Company B; Pvt. Elijah N. Freeman, Company B; Cpl. Lafayette Frost, Company A; Pvt. John Green, Company C; Pvt. James Hampton, Company A; Pvt. Milton Kelley, Company E; Pvt. Melcher Oyler, Company A; Pvt. John Perkins, Company C; Pvt. Alva Phelps, Company E; Musician Joseph W. Richards, Company A; 3rd Cpl. James A. Scott, Company E; Pvt. Norman Sharp, Company D; Pvt. David Smith, Company E; and 1st Cpl. Arnold Stephens, Company D.

Three additional battalion men were killed by Indians following their discharge while crossing the Sierra Nevada Mountains: musician Ezra H. Allen, Company C; Sgt. Daniel Browett, Company E; and Pvt. Henderson Cox, Company A; John and Jane Boscoe, an older couple with Capt. Jefferson Hunt, both died on the Arkansas River (Kansas) on August 27 and 30, 1846, respectively. Tyler specifies their deaths as being August 28 and 29 (*Concise History*, 142); Parley Hunt, infant son of Capt. Jefferson Hunt, died at Pueblo; Fent Allred, a child, died between Santa Fe and Pueblo; Betsy Prescinda Huntington, a child, died at Pueblo; a private teamster for Capt. Daniel C. Davis, Elisha Smith, died near Ash Creek, New Mexico, December 5, 1846; Lydia Ann Edmonds Hunter, wife of Capt. Jesse D. Hunter, died at San Diego on April 27, 1847, and was buried on Point Loma on the Fort Rosecrans Military Reservation; Maj. Jeremiah H. Cloud died near Sutter's Fort, August 4, 1847. The march of the battalion and later garrison duty in the respective locations were not without significant sacrifice of human life, and the names of those who died are held in "honorable remembrance" (see military and family records in possession of writer); Elmer J. Carr, ed., *Honorable Remembrance: The San Diego Master List of the Mormon Battalion* (San Diego: Mormon Battalion Visitors' Center, 1978), 74–80, 90–97; Carl V. Larson, comp. and ed., *A Data Base of the Mormon Battalion*, 2nd ed. (Salt Lake City: U.S. Mormon Battalion, 1997); Norma Baldwin Ricketts, *The Mormon Battalion* (Logan: Utah State University Press, 1996); Carl V. Larson and Shirley N. Maynes, eds., *Women of the Mormon Battalion* (n.p.: ABC Printing, 1997), 124, 126–27; Dan Talbot, *A Historical Guide to the Mormon Battalion and Butterfield Trail* (Tucson: Westernlore Press, 1992), 103–13.

13. Tyler, *Concise History*, 134.

14. James S. Brown, *Life of a Pioneer* (Salt Lake City: George Q. Cannon & Sons, 1900), 29.

15. Tyler, *Concise History*, 136.

16. Journal History, August 11, 1846.

17. Journal History, August 21, 1846; Watson, *Manuscript History of Brigham Young*, 344.

18. Tyler, *Concise History*, 136.

19. Frank Alfred Golder, comp., *The March of the Mormon Battalion from Council Bluffs to California Taken from the Journal of Henry Standage* (New York: Century, 1928), 146.

20. Journal of Samuel Hollister Rogers, August 20, 1846, 57, typescript, 79–80, L. Tom Perry Special Collections, Harold B. Lee Library, Brigham Young University, Provo, Utah.

21. Journal of William Hyde, August 26, 1846, 19, Church Archives, The Church of Jesus Christ of Latter-day Saints, Salt Lake City.

22. Tyler, *Concise History*, 143–44.

23. Yurtinus, "A Ram in the Thicket," 1:122–26; Tyler, *Concise History*, 147.

24. Tyler, *Concise History*, 150.

25. Journal History, September 14, 1846. The research of Mary Lindenmuth Scarcello has produced a larger figure than the forty-three persons suggested by William Crosby. She has identified some eighty-five persons who were associated with the "Mississippi Company" during its tenure at the fort. However, her research includes bond servants, children born at the site, and perhaps other categories of people who interacted with the company during the period of occupancy and were not part of the Crosby count (see Mary Linenmuth Scarcello, *Mormon Pioneers in Pueblo, Colorado, 1846–1900* [n.d.: Mary Lindenmuth Scarcello, 1993], 119–52).

26. Scarcello, *Mormon Pioneers in Pueblo*, 31–33, 119–52.

27. Journal History, September 16, 1846; Tyler, *Concise History*, 158.

28. Captain Nelson Higgins and those able-bodied men who formed the escort to Pueblo rejoined the Battalion at Santa Fe. Since Colonel Philip St. George Cooke had already left for the Rio Grande, the commander at Santa Fe directed Captain Higgins and his men to serve on detached duty in Pueblo with the stipulation that they would provide for their families there (see Yurtinus, "A Ram in the Thicket," 1:263).

29. For a complete listing of personnel comprising the Capt. Nelson Higgins detachment from the Arkansas River to Pueblo, September 16, 1846, see author's original article in Boone, *Regional Studies*.

30. Tyler, *Concise History*, 159.

31. George Rutledge Gibson, *Journal of a Soldier under Kearny and Doniphan, 1846–47*, ed. Ralph P. Bieber, *The Southwest Historical Series* (Glendale, CA: Arthur K. Clark, 1935), 3:252.

32. Stephen W. Kearny, Orders No. 33, October 3, 1846, Headquarters, Army of the West, Camp on the Rio Del Norte near Joya, Church Archives.

33. "Orders No. 8," in Tyler, *Concise History*, 166–68.

34. For a complete listing of personnel comprising the Capt. James Brown detachment from Santa Fe to Pueblo, October 18, 1846, see author's original article in Boone, *Regional Studies*.

35. He is listed as "Bowing" on the reenlistment company muster roll and as "Boring" on a document in William Hunter's pension file

36. Family records in possession of writer; Tyler, *Concise History*, 125; Carr, *Honorable Remembrance*, 88; Ricketts, *Mormon Battalion*, 280–81; Larson, *Data Base of the Mormon Battalion*, 30, 69, 182–84, 219. Nathan Young's Pension File stipulates he was a servant to Capt. Jesse D. Hunter (see letter of F. H. Morris, Auditor, War Department, March 28, 1900).

37. Order No. 16, see Journal History, November 10, 1846.

38. Journal of Levi W. Hancock, November 10, 1846, Church Archives.

39. For a complete listing of personnel comprising the Lt. William W. Willis detachment from the Rio Grande to Pueblo, November 10, 1846, see author's original article in Boone, *Regional Studies*.

40. Yurtinus, "A Ram in the Thicket," 1:287–88; Tyler, *Concise History*, 192.

41. For a complete listing of the men of the Mormon Battalion who continued the march to California from the Rio Grande, see author's original article in Boone, *Regional Studies*.

42. Cooke, "Cooke's Journal," 70, 74, 85–86, 107, 175–76, 201; Yurtinus, "A Ram in the Thicket," 1:190, 230; 2:345, 357, 372, 395, 401; Carr, *Honorable Remembrance*, 68–70.

43. Tyler, *Concise History*, 218–19.

44. Yurtinus, "A Ram in the Thicket," 2:405–13.

45. Yurtinus, "A Ram in the Thicket," 2:413–17.

46. Tyler, *Concise History*, 236.

47. James H. McClintock, *Mormon Settlement in Arizona* (Phoenix: Manufacturing Stationers, 1921).

48. Cooke, "Cooke's Journal," 233–34.

49. Samuel H. Rodgers, "Samuel H. Rodgers Diary," January 27, 1847, 114, L. Tom Perry Special Collections.

50. Cooke, "Cooke's Journal," 235–36.

51. Diary of Henry G. Boyle, January 27, 1847, 34, typescript, L. Tom Perry Special Collections.

52. Diary of Henry G. Boyle, 35.

53. Golder, *March of the Mormon Battalion*, 208–10; Robert S. Bliss, "Journal of Robert Bliss," 86, Church Archives; Henry W. Bigler Diary, February 3, 1847, typescript, 63, L. Tom Perry Special Collections.

54. Cooke, "Cooke's Journal," 238–40; emphasis added.

55. Diary of Redick N. Allred, December 19, 1847, in Kate B. Carter, comp., *Treasures of Pioneer History* (Salt Lake City: Daughters of Utah Pioneers, 1956), 5:310.

Introduction to the Utah War

"WOUNDED, NONE; KILLED, NONE:
FOOLED, EVERYBODY."
—*Captain Jesse Gove, 10th U.S. Infantry,
regarding the Utah War*

★ ★ ★

KNOWN POPULARLY AMONG STUDENTS of U.S. history and Latter-day Saints as Buchanan's Blunder, the Mormon War, Johnston's Army, or the Utah Expedition, this conflict is perhaps more correctly called the Utah War of 1857–58. Prior to the onslaught of the American Civil War (1861–65), the federal government and the Latter-day Saints of Utah Territory locked horns in a political, diplomatic, and legal struggle beginning in the early 1850s, which culminated in a military showdown in the fall of 1857. Though no one died in a traditional armed battle, the Utah War was not bloodless—dozens of innocent people loss their lives through indirect forces caused by the Utah War.

From the time Utah became an official federal territory in 1850, conflict grew between the Saints and the government's appointed officials. To most Americans, the Mormons of the Great Basin were a troublesome lot—strange, fanatical, heretical, and too far outside the mainstream of nineteenth-century America. The Saints, in contrast, felt betrayed and persecuted by their fellow Americans and saw themselves as victims of religious persecution in the land of liberty. These attitudes and differences lay at the core of the conflict and had earlier emerged in the violence of "Bleeding Kansas" and the clamor for states' rights and popular sovereignty. The war in Utah may not have been a contest by a more traditional or classical definition, but to the Saints it was a war they were willing to fight if necessary.

> The war of words and attitudes nearly erupted into combat.

After years of receiving official reports, letters, newspaper accounts, and direct testimony accusing Latter-day Saint leaders of sedition and religious tyranny, the federal government demanded Brigham Young's replacement as territorial governor and the establishment of a less "theocratic" government in this wayward territory. President James Buchanan ordered a military force to escort the new federal officials and to establish and enforce federal law. The war of words and attitudes nearly erupted into combat as Latter-day Saint militia destroyed provisions and captured army stock—acts of open rebellion against federal authority. Not willing to submit without a demonstration of defiance, Brigham Young essentially waved a clenched fist at Uncle Sam but simultaneously sent messengers to negotiate a peaceful arrangement in Washington. The U.S. government had no pretense or anticipation of actual hostilities as the army advanced toward Utah, and it was caught unaware, a dismal showing for the professional regular army. Yet near an oasis along the southern migration route in southern Utah, hysterical Mormon militia and others decided on a dreadful course at Mountain Meadows that culminated in a heart-breaking massacre.

By 1858, adversaries of the Saints saw the foolishness of civil war and negotiated peace and a pardon. For the next three years, an occupying force based in Utah caused few actual problems but incensed the Saints. When the Civil War began in 1861, the regular army closed its largest post in the West and returned to enter the bloodbath in the East.

The Utah War has great significance for Americans as perhaps the first armed contest between a U.S. territory and federal authority. The war represented the largest military operation between the Mexican War and the Civil War; during the Utah War a fourth of the regular army was stationed in Utah.

3

The Church and the Utah War, 1857–58

SHERMAN L. FLEEK

✶ ✶ ✶

THE UTAH WAR WAS DIFFERENT from any other military conflict or venture in which members of The Church of Jesus Christ of Latter-day Saints have participated. In subsequent wars and military expeditions—with the exception of the Civil War—the Church and its members have supported and fought for the United States and other nations' armed forces to defeat other enemies. In the Utah War, however, this was not the case. In acts of self-preservation, the Church and the

*Lieutenant Colonel Sherman L. Fleek,
United States Army (retired), is a former chief historian
for the National Guard Bureau.*

Lot Smith (1830–92)

At the young age of sixteen, Lot Smith volunteered to be a member of the Mormon Battalion. The experience and knowledge he gained on this overland march to California would prove invaluable to the Church for many years to come. Upon returning to Salt Lake, Smith became a leader in the Nauvoo Legion. During the Utah War, Major Smith carried out his orders to impede the progress of the army while also following the order not to hurt anyone except in self-defense.

Lot Smith. Courtesy of Church Archives.

At the outbreak of the Civil War, Lot Smith was again called upon to participate in a military role. He was assigned with one hundred men to protect the telegraph lines, the mail lines, and any settlers traveling from St. Louis to Salt Lake City. His success earned him great acclaim from his peers and other federal cavalry units.

After the Civil War, Smith was called by Brigham Young to aid in the colonization efforts of the Church. He was sent to Arizona to help establish settlements there. In June 1892, he was killed by a renegade Native American in Tuba City, Arizona (Arnold K. Garr, Donald Q. Cannon, and Richard O. Cowan, eds., *Encyclopedia of Latter-day Saint History* [Salt Lake City: Deseret Book, 2000], 1134–35).

Territory of Utah openly challenged federal authority and conducted military operations against the U.S. Army. The territorial militia, known as the Nauvoo Legion, destroyed valuable U.S. military provisions and supplies and stole government livestock, stopping just short of engaging in combat. Thus, the Utah War is a unique military experience in Church history.

During most wars, Church membership has grown and lands have been opened to missionary opportunities in the aftermath of war. Similarly, in most conflicts, the Church has supported national war efforts through nonmilitary means by donating food, goods, and money to ease the pain of those affected by the war.

During the Utah War, these future trends did not apply. Instead of increasing missionary opportunities, Church colonies and settlements closed; missions were terminated; calls to new missionaries stopped; work on the Salt Lake Temple ceased and the foundation was buried; food and resources were hoarded and not allowed to be sold to non–Latter-day Saint immigrant trains; shops and manufacturing entities produced war materiel as opposed to consumer goods; and most of the population of the northern Utah cities left their homes and property and moved south to Utah Valley for several weeks in 1858.

In fact, during the spring of 1858, residents of Salt Lake City had prepared to destroy their city rather than allow the U.S. Army to occupy it. During the Utah War the most dreadful event in Church history occurred—the Mountain Meadows Massacre. This tragedy occurred as an act related to war hysteria generated during the Utah War, which led some Latter-day Saints to become crazed in their zeal against their perceived enemies.[1] The Utah War was different from any other armed conflict the Church experienced.

Significance of the Utah War

Commonly called the "Utah Expedition" in official military and government sources, the title "Utah War" more accurately captures the broad scope of this political, economic, military, and religious conflict. It has come to represent the first major rebellion against federal authority by a political entity, the Utah Territory. In a sense, this conflict foreshadowed the Civil War (1861–65), when the Southern states rebelled against the Federal Union. Many of the political and ethical issues that were center stage in 1860 during the secession crisis were first addressed in Utah in the 1850s. Chief among them was the question of supremacy between state and national governments.

The exercise of federal authority in Utah was unlike federal responses to earlier revolts in American history, such as Shays's Rebellion in 1786–87 in New England and the Whiskey Rebellion of 1794 in the western Pennsylvania and Ohio Valley areas.[2] These earlier uprisings were led by common citizens, not by local or state government entities. During the Nullification Crisis of 1832, the state of South Carolina challenged the tariff law, but when President

The Mountain Meadows Massacre

One of the darkest days in Utah and Mormon history occurred during the Utah War period. On September 11, 1857, more than a hundred innocent men, women, and children in the Baker-Fancher party, mostly from Arkansas, were slaughtered as they crossed southern Utah on their way to California. Mormon militia, primarily members of the Nauvoo Legion, and Paiute Indians were involved in this tragedy. Some historians, including Juanita Brooks, consider the prime cause of this problem to be the war hysteria local citizens felt as federal troops were marching to Utah with unstated intentions. Other historians paint a picture of conspiracy in the Church.

It is impossible to know all the events, decisions, and men involved in this brutal crime. The Baker-Fancher party did, in fact, surrender to Mormon militia leaders after four days of siege by Paiutes, as they supposed, but in reality most of the attackers were from the militia. The party was lined up and marched out in the desert plain near Mountain Meadows, a favorite water stop along the Old Spanish Trail. There, militia members and Indians fell upon the unarmed party and killed them. Only seventeen small children were spared.

The conspirators swore oaths of secrecy, and for years many held the sorrow of that day in their hearts. Eventually some confessed, and one leader, Major John D. Lee, was tried and executed for his role in the massacre. Many others could have faced the same justice.

Many historians and others have tried to connect Brigham Young and Church headquarters to this dreadful act, but only speculation and circumstantial pieces support this position. It would have been quite uncharacteristic of Brigham Young to order or approve such a massacre. With an army of U.S. regulars en route to Utah and with Utah's inadequate resources of war materiel, why would he approve of the massacre of an unarmed wagon train? Several immigrant trains passed through Utah that year, and some traveled by the same route after the massacre, so why kill the Baker-Fancher party? The most reasonable answer lies with the hysteria of local citizens and their fear of upcoming war. Thus, the Utah War, which is remembered for avoidance of all-out conflict with federal troops, is darkened by the tragedy of the Mountain Meadows Massacre.

Andrew Jackson threatened the use of federal troops, state officials relented.[3] These other conflicts were either local popular contentions or political disputes, as in the Nullification Crisis. After the conflict in Utah ended, President James Buchanan issued pardons to individuals in Utah Territory who had participated in open rebellion and destroyed government property.[4] Utah rebelled only after regular army troops were involved and had entered Utah Territory.

What is most interesting historically is the nature and status of Brigham Young as both the head of Utah's dominant religion and the chief executive of the government body. He was more than just a deeply religious person in a public office of great trust—he was the head of a church in an area where the vast majority of the body politic were members of that church. Furthermore, it was more than just a normal, nineteenth-century American sect that Young headed. The Church claimed divine authority and viewed its head, who was also governor of Utah, as more than just a theological leader but as a prophet of God in every sense of the biblical definition. Brigham Young was the theological, ecclesiastical, cultural, legal, military, and political executive of life in Utah Territory. To the eastern political establishment, he was an American pope reigning over a federal entity in the West. This alone caused great alarm in Washington and among the American public.[5]

As the first Anglo-American settlers in the Great Basin, Latter-day Saints sought to establish political control and power for themselves. This basic desire to govern themselves with limited or no interference from any outside influence largely precipitated the Utah War. Unlike states' rights as defined later by Southern agitators—with state authority being superior to federal authority—Utah wanted local control by filling federal judgeships and positions by local people and not outsiders.

The conflict was the largest and most prominent military operation to occur between the Mexican (1846–48) and Civil wars.

Dozens of officers from the Utah campaign served as generals during the Civil War. The Utah War was a valuable training and leadership exercise for the war in the East and for frontier campaigns for decades to come. For example, army captain Randolph Marcy's overland mission in winter through treacherous mountains and severe deserts of the American West was a marvel of leadership, discipline, and fortitude. He led a few dozen soldiers and frontiersmen through the southwest corner of future Wyoming, into eastern Utah, and then into New Mexico to secure necessary provisions and livestock for the Utah column.[6]

> The political issue of the proper use of military forces in Utah serves as another fascinating lesson for what not to do.

Military logistics is an area in which the U.S. military provided a textbook example of how not to conduct a campaign—crossing a thousand miles of frontier during the late season. The political issue of the proper use of military forces in Utah serves as another fascinating lesson for what not to do. Later the issue of using regular army forces as a posse comitatus and as a police constabulary during the Reconstruction era was an intense emotional problem for Southerners. American government later developed policies and laws for military activity as a result of lessons learned from the Utah War. Because the Utah episode occurred just before the major conflict of Southern rebellion and also because it was a bloodless campaign, most Americans today do not know much of this unique military, political, and social clash.

Brigham Young, circa 1850. Courtesy of Church Archives.

Prologue

To truly understand the conditions out of which the Utah War arose, one must briefly consider the Latter-day Saint story before 1857 or even before the Saints entered the Great Basin in 1847. The story begins with Joseph Smith, the founder of The Church of Jesus Christ of Latter-day Saints and one of the most significant characters in American religious experience. Under his leadership, the Church experienced nearly two decades of tremendous doctrinal development and membership growth, leading up to the exodus to the Rocky Mountains. The Saints endured years of persistent persecution before arriving in what would become Utah.

The persecutions occurred during the heady days of Jacksonian democracy. It is not my purpose to recount or narrate this tragic chapter in Mormon and American history in full, but it is important to understand the situation of a people who were forced from several eastern and midwestern states; whose fellow Church members were murdered; whose homes and property were destroyed or stolen by their neighbors; who lost whole communities they had carved out of wilderness; and who were deprived of two majestic temples—their sacred centers of worship.

Ironically, even as these religious fugitives fled to the western mountains, they carried a love for the principles of the United States and a dedication to the dreams and rights established by its founders, though at the time many were angry with the U.S. government for its inaction on their behalf. Many Saints were convinced during the Utah War that they were the true guardians of Constitutional rights, freedoms, and American values.

By 1857 some forty thousand Saints, mostly from eastern states and Europe, had created dozens of communities in their "Zion."[7] The Saints struggled for years to make life pleasant and bountiful in a harsh, arid climate, and their success was modest at best. Beyond making the desert into a garden, Brigham Young and the Saints sought isolation from governmental and societal influences and powers beyond their control.[8] But geography forced other qualities onto the separate kingdom of the Saints. Utah grew and prospered somewhat from gold mining in California and other western locales, which brought tens of thousands of fortune seekers and others through Utah. Army expeditions and surveys, scientific explorers, and federal officials came also.

An Unlikely Convert

Charles Henry Wilcken, first a member of Johnston's Army, later joined The Church of Jesus Christ of Latter-day Saints. Wilcken, having earned distinction in the Prussian army during the Schleswig-Holstein wars of the late 1840s, had sought a new life and new adventures. While initial plans called for the German-born Wilcken to travel elsewhere, he arrived in New York in the spring of 1857, anticipating exciting adventure. He soon realized that his life was simply a struggle for survival. Not fluent in English and unable to find employment, a penniless Wilcken walked into an army recruiting office and joined. Recruitment had been active in hopes of raising an army to be sent west to put down a supposed uprising of Mormons.

Charles Henry Wilcken. Courtesy of Church Archives.

While he was unsure of who Mormons were, Wilcken was intrigued at the fervor that had been ignited by their activities. He quickly became disgusted by the American army, its lack of organization, training, and discipline, as well as the seeming lack of moral character exhibited by its troops. Having come from the most organized and professional army in the world, he was appalled by the stark contrast he saw around him. By the time the army had reached the Wyoming plains, Wilcken decided his time with the army had come to an end. Having been instructed to do so in a dream, he approached his commanding officer with the request to spend the day hunting. Granted permission, he set off. Feeling guided in his journey, he soon met members of Major Lot Smith's cavalry and was taken captive.

His captors, however, surprised him. They were very friendly and even allowed him to retain his uniform and weapons, asking for his assistance in herding several hundred head of cattle down the canyon. Upon reaching the valley, Wilcken was warmly welcomed and put into the care of the bishop of Provo. Not long after, he was baptized a member. He spent several years in Heber, where he was able to bring his wife and small children from Germany, and assist in training the local militia. He received a mission call to Germany in 1869 but was delayed two years over concerns of his being arrested on his journey as a deserter from the army. This situation was remedied when he received an official affidavit attesting to his having been captured by Mormon militia during the Utah campaign.

After his mission, Wilcken became one of Salt Lake City's first police officers and was later called to serve as a bodyguard for President John Taylor and later President Wilford Woodruff. He was instrumental in helping keep these brethren and many others protected from federal prosecution for practicing polygamy (Charles Henry Wilcken Papers, courtesy of the Wilcken family).

Causes and Reactions

Thus, after a quarter century of existence and ten years of unsteady peace and prosperity in the mountains and Great Basin, the Saints were determined to stay; to maintain their communities, homes, families; and, if necessary, to fight to guarantee their rights, property, and religious freedom.

Perhaps the two main factors that caused the Utah War can best be summarized as first, the differences in policies between federal and Church authorities concerning relations with the Utah Indians. The second consisted of Americans' absolute fear of Mormon power and religious teachings, including such practices as polygamy, combined with the fear of perceived Mormon vigilantism and oppression of non-Mormons. Of course, most Latter-day Saints then and now would consider these charges absurd. Still, both were allegedly manifest at the Mountain Meadows Massacre.[9]

In the ten years since arriving in the Great Basin, these American settlers had established dozens of communities and settlements, organized a territorial government with Congressional approval, developed an agricultural society and rudiments of its economic foundation, sought to live in harmony with Native Americans, and allowed other Americans to travel through the territory on their way to California or Oregon. Historian Norman Furniss wrote, "One basic cause of the difficulties throughout this decade, and indeed in later years, was the existence of a public opinion extremely hostile to the Mormons and prepared to seize upon any pretext, whether valid or not, to renew the attack upon the Church."[10]

Some non-Mormons stayed in the territory, although Indian relations were unstable and occasionally violent, but tens of thousands of American and European converts flocked to "Zion" for safety and community.[11] The fact that the Saints also publicly practiced plural marriage brought intense criticism from other Americans.

Federal appointees and military parties, arriving in Utah between 1848 and 1856, sought to fulfill directives and missions of the national government. Relations between these officials and the Latter-day Saints soon deteriorated into accusations, insults, and a substantial breakdown of official authority and trust. Some of these officials fled the territory, spreading exaggerated stories and accusations against the Mormons and their religious theocracy. The Mormons, indeed, had developed their own local courts and authority outside the established practices in other states and territories. Some of this governmental apparatus predated the Utah experience of the Saints. The probate courts, which often resembled a religious judicial process, caused great anxiety among territorial judges.

> **Though the Utah appointees were not prime selections for offices in government, neither were they the villains that legend and some histories have caricatured them.**

Latter-day Saint culture tended to exclude non-Mormons from many facets of the community, partly from their past experience and partly from a sense of religious superiority. However, this practice has often been richly exaggerated in literature and history from the early Utah period. "If the Mormon leaders did not encourage intimidation and violence against both gentiles and apostates," wrote historian Robert Coakley, "they seldom took any action to punish the perpetrators of such acts and frustrated the efforts of gentile federal judges to do so. In short, the Mormons made it practically impossible for federal officials to operate in Utah who were unsympathetic to

Mormons control of the territory."[12] Mormon attitude provided its own unique style of drawing a line in the sand. Leading the charge was Brigham Young, who felt that his office as governor was just as religious in nature as his Church position. "I am and will be Governor, and no power can hinder it, until the Lord Almighty says, 'Brigham, you need not be Governor any longer,' and then I am willing to yield to another Governor."[13]

Though the Utah appointees were not prime selections for offices in government, neither were they the villains that legend and some histories have caricatured them. In many cases they were federal officials trying to conduct business among people who were skeptical and sometimes hostile to their actions.

The territorial judges, Indian agents, and other officials allowed their hatred of Mormon practices, unity, and religious zeal to cloud their judgment of the true nature of conditions in Utah during the 1850s. Most of these officials fled Utah because of perceived threats against them. Some of the complaints had a basis in fact, because the Mormons generally did refuse to subordinate themselves to the judges and U.S. marshals. The situation deteriorated into a hopeless morass in which neither party could see or understand the truth of conditions, politics, justice, and law in Utah. The Saints felt they were victims persecuted by wicked federal conspirators, whereas the officials saw Mormon authority as a manifestation of religious extremism.[14]

Into this vortex of national issues, including state (territorial) rights, abolition, free soil, free labor, and the violence in "Bleeding Kansas," Utah entered the national scene. Yet many Americans saw their unique rights and values threatened by a close-knit, fanatical theocracy that seemed to trample the Constitution under their growing numbers and threatened to control local politics. The perception of Mormon hegemony caused great turmoil and distrust among American citizens who had often lived for years in these regions and states.

The American public's fear of Mormon teachings and practices should not be ignored. As the western migration through lands inhabited by native tribes continued, the Mormons seemed to be uniting with the Indians against other Americans. As misguided as these sentiments may appear today, they were real perceptions then. Just as real were the Latter-day Saints concerns over judicial proceedings, representation in Congress, land ownership, and mail delivery. These issues caused raw emotion among the Saints.

May to August 1857

After years of complaints, letters, reports, and a dozen or so affidavits from so-called runaway officials and army officers, President Buchanan decided it was time to act. The government had been severely abused by the press for its inaction in "Bleeding Kansas" the year before. It should be noted that Buchanan was later criticized for issues relating to the beginnings of the Civil War at Fort Sumter.[15] The president, on the advice of a few advisers, determined that Utah Territory was in rebellion against federal power. He based his decision on allegations that judicial records had been burned and on the treatment of officials in general. For example, Almon W. Babbitt, Utah secretary of state, was murdered in 1856 by Indians, not on Brigham Young's orders, as often cited. Allegations of interference of Latter-day Saints with U.S. mail were perceived as another assault on governmental power.

Unfortunately, many of these attitudes and accusations were circulated in newspapers and press releases in the East. Some of the runaway officials, such as Judge William W. Drummond, took delight in exacerbating these issues. Dr. Garland Hurt, a former Indian agent and perhaps the most reasonable and the longest-serving government official in this period, also turned against the Latter-day Saints and denounced the relationships the Saints had with the Native Americans. These types of public and official accusations led the

Camp Floyd

Camp Floyd (named for John B. Floyd, secretary of war) was established by Colonel Albert Sidney Johnston at the conclusion of the Utah War. Brigham Young requested that it be no closer than forty miles from any major Latter-day Saint settlement. It was established on the west side of Utah Lake and is maintained today as a state park. Camp Floyd was one of the most important government installations in the years before the Civil War. It housed the Utah Department and was the largest military garrison in the nation, with approximately 3,500 troops. Though Utah was never the site of any Civil War battles, Camp Floyd was a training ground for the soldiers. Fifty-nine of its officers later served as generals in the Civil War. Interestingly, thirty of the future generals fought for the Union and twenty-nine for the Confederacy (*Deseret News*, October 28, 2005).

By 1860 the fort had been renamed Camp Crittenden, and command was given to Colonel Philip St. George Cooke, friend of the Saints and former leader of the Mormon Battalion. As tension between the North and South increased, the military complement of Fort Crittenden was cut to around seven hundred troops. A month after the war began, Colonel Cooke was ordered to dismantle the fort, sell off all supplies, and immediately bring his command east. This proved a blessing to the Saints as they purchased over four million dollars' worth of supplies and equipment for pennies on the dollar. As a final act before the troops left the valley, Colonel Cooke had the camp's flagpole installed in front of Brigham Young's home as a gift (Audrey M. Godfrey, www.media.utah.edu/UHE/c/CAMPFLOYD.html; accessed October 18, 2006).

Republican Party to denounce the twin relics of barbarism, "slavery and polygamy," in its presidential election in 1856. Even former friend and judge Stephen A. Douglas, then a U.S. senator for Illinois, condemned the Mormons as a cancer that had to be removed from the body politic.[16]

President Buchanan, acting with uncharacteristic resolve, asked Secretary of War John B. Floyd and General Winfield Scott to consider organizing a military escort for the new federal officials' move to Utah. The military was to establish order and enforce the laws of the United States and to impose martial law upon the territory if necessary. Thus, a posse comitatus principle was approved so that even the federal judges could exercise control over U.S. troops.[17]

President Brigham Young, of course, knew of the difficult relations between his people and the federal officials, but he and his followers generally labeled the problems as religious persecution. He was not aware

The remustered Nauvoo Legion. Courtesy of Church Archives.

that a new governor was en route to replace him and that a small army was going to enforce national authority. The first indication of a gathering storm was the termination of the mail contract with the U.S. Post Office in the spring of 1857.[18]

On July 24, 1857, ten years to the day after Brigham Young entered the valley, thousands of Saints were in the mountains celebrating the anniversary when riders brought word that a military force was en route to Utah. For the next few weeks, Young and his advisers discussed the meaning of the government's actions without any word from national officials.[19]

It became obvious that stringent policies were needed to safeguard the settlements and the Saints' property and lives. Food, a bartering commodity with immigrant trains, was restricted for sale to Church members only. Full reorganization of Utah's militia, the Nauvoo Legion, continued an effort that had actually begun months earlier. Weapons and gunpowder were stockpiled. In order to arm the legion, revolvers and other firearms were produced locally, some even on Temple Square itself. At its height, the Nauvoo Legion could field and equip only a fraction of the four thousand

The Church and the Utah War, 1857–58 ★ 95

men on the muster rolls. Organized into military divisions, normally by county, the legion was commanded by General Daniel Wells, a member of the First Presidency. General Wells was an accomplished leader, businessman, and Church officer, but he had no military experience beyond militia service.

The legion's only real military experience belonged to a few hundred members who had served ten years earlier in the Mormon Battalion, which had never engaged in combat. With inexperienced leadership in training and combat operations, a limited number of firearms, no useful artillery, inadequate equipment, and little time to train and prepare, the Latter-day Saint military force faced a daunting challenge. Their only advantages were their knowledge of the terrain, a strong base of logistical operations, and support from their local populace.

The only logical course of action for the Saints was to conduct a guerilla campaign, as opposed to direct conventional combat, and to use the land, weather, and stealth in their favor. Other actions taken as the conflict continued included recalling missionaries from abroad and closing remote and far-flung settlements. At the same time, food, equipment, fodder for animals, and all valuable stores were safeguarded for family and community needs.

Fortunately, during this time two important events increased the Saints' chances of survival. First, they started an all-out campaign to encourage local Native American tribes to ally themselves with the Mormons against "Gentiles," whose treatment of the tribes was worse than the more benign treatment by Mormons. Second, senior leaders traveled among the settlements giving intense and emotional speeches to boost morale and prepare the Saints for the most dire possibilities.[20]

Out in the field, Church leaders preached and exhorted their fellow Saints to prepare for any contingency, especially war against the United States.[21] From Salt Lake City in the Old Tabernacle and other locations, Apostles chastised those who wavered in the faith.

Albert Sidney Johnston (1803–62)

Before rising to the position of commander of the Utah Expedition, Albert Sidney Johnston fought during the Texas War of Independence and at Monterrey during the Mexican-American War. In truth, the Saints were fortunate that Johnston had been given command of the Utah Expedition. Johnston was more moderate in his approach to the "Utah problem" than his predecessor, General William Harney. Even with this tempered attitude, General Johnston was not a friend of the Church. After entering the Salt Lake Valley, he commented that he "would give up his plantation for a chance to bombard the city for 15 minutes." His service during the Utah Expedition earned him the brevet rank of brigadier general, and after several years in command of the Utah Department at Camp Floyd he was given command of the Department of the Pacific in California.

Albert Sidney Johnston.
Courtesy of Church Archives.

At the onset of the Civil War, Johnston left his post and traveled to Richmond, Virginia, to offer his services to the new Confederacy. He was immediately promoted to the second-highest rank in the Confederate Army and given command of the Western Department. Confederate President Jefferson Davis and some officials in the Confederate government considered Johnston to be one of the most competent officers and military minds in the Confederate Army.

General Johnston immediately set up a line of defense from the Appalachians in Kentucky to the Mississippi River. This line proved inadequate, however, and Johnston's armies suffered a series of humiliating defeats at the hands of General Ulysses S. Grant. His army was forced to retreat into northern Mississippi to regroup.

In the spring of 1862, Johnston's army led a surprise attack against General Grant's forces at Shiloh. The attack caught the Union forces completely unaware and proved successful. While leading the charge on the Union position General Johnston was shot behind the knee. Because he did not feel the wound was serious, Johnston sent his personal physician away to aid other wounded enemy troops and continued to lead his men. Minutes later, his staff noticed that he appeared quite faint. When asked if he was wounded, he replied, "Yes, and I fear seriously," before toppling from his horse. The bullet had ruptured an artery in his leg, and his boot had begun to fill with blood. He bled to death within minutes and became the highest-ranking casualty of the Civil War.

Young's close friend and counselor President Heber C. Kimball explained the moral authority that the prophet carried: "Our Father and our God has sent Brigham and his brethren; if you rebel against them, you rebel against the authority that sent them."[22] Such pronouncements clarified for the Saints to whom they should look for direction during the tumultuous months ahead.

The Utah Army Organized and on the March

By May 1857, President Buchanan had ordered Secretary Floyd and General Scott to dispatch a military force to accompany the territorial governor and newly appointed federal officials to Utah. Scott knew that the small regular army was already stretched to its limit, given its far-flung missions from Florida to California, including patrolling war-torn "Bleeding Kansas." Scott first estimated that the Latter-day Saints could not field more than four thousand effective troops—a number that proved very realistic.[23] Therefore, Scott ordered some two thousand five hundred soldiers—two regiments of infantry (eight companies of the Tenth Infantry and all ten companies of the Fifth Infantry) and a strong cavalry support of six, later eight, companies of the Second Dragoons. Also ordered were two batteries of artillery—one each from the Fourth and Fifth Artillery Regiments. These units joined the command at Fort Leavenworth, the base of operations. The army was now a brigade-sized force and was the largest military operation between the Mexican and Civil wars. Command of the campaign was given to General William Harney of Louisiana.[24]

Floyd ordered the military bureaus under his, not Scott's, control, to prepare logistics and contracts for moving and supplying a major military force one thousand two hundred miles across the frontier. Floyd arranged for the Quartermaster Department to send an officer in advance of the main column to secure provisions,

The army faced a difficult and bitter winter on the Wyoming plains. *Never a Complaint*, by Don Stivers. Courtesy of Don Stivers.

locate a suitable camp site, and arrange for services among the Mormons.[25] This advance party, led by Captain Stewart Van Vliet of the Quartermaster Department, became the most obvious symbol that the federal government did not desire a hostile conflict with the Saints. If the army leadership contemplated war and combat, then sending a small detachment under Captain Van Vliet was both risky and foolish. Greeted with guarded hospitality, Church leaders made a determined plea to Van Vliet that they had been wronged by the government and that Utah Territory was not in rebellion, yet they would defend themselves and their homes.[26]

Thomas L. Kane (1822–83)

Thomas L. Kane, born in Philadelphia, son of a wealthy lawyer, was himself trained as a lawyer and was well educated, having attended school in Philadelphia, England, and France. Kane's relationship with the Church began in May 1846 during a special conference of the Church held in Philadelphia by Elder Jesse C. Little. After the conference, Kane invited Elder Little to his home, where they discussed the issues surrounding the expulsion of the Saints from Nauvoo and their desire to migrate farther west. Kane wrote several letters of introduction for Elder Little to use in petitioning the government for assistance. Kane later joined Elder Little in meetings with President James K. Polk. It was Thomas Kane who was able to convince President Polk to ask for a company of Mormon volunteers for the war with Mexico. With his curiosity of the Church piqued, Kane traveled and met the Saints on the banks of the Missouri. There he met with Brigham Young and other Church leaders and quickly won their friendship.

While returning to Philadelphia, Kane visited Nauvoo and traveled through Missouri to personally witness the deprivations and persecutions the Saints had suffered. Deeply moved by what he saw, he vowed from that day to be a sincere friend of the Latter-day Saints. Later, when the Utah Territory was organized, U. S. officials asked Thomas Kane to be the first territorial governor. He politely declined but suggested that Brigham Young be appointed instead.

When word reached Salt Lake City of the approaching federal army, Brigham Young instructed elders in the east to ask Kane for help in contacting the government to address the many misunderstandings that had led to hostilities. Kane immediately went to work contacting his many influential friends. He offered his services to President Polk as mediator to the conflict and was granted permission to go but was told that though he had the president's confidence he would receive no official status as mediator. Undaunted, Kane traveled to California by ship under an assumed name and quietly entered the Salt Lake Valley with a group of Latter-day Saint emigrants. Kane was able to effectively and efficiently organize a peaceful settlement between Brigham Young and the federal authorities. He arranged to have the newly appointed governor enter Salt Lake City unescorted. This peaceful transition prompted the new governor to write Washington and request that the military campaign end.

Thomas L. Kane

Thomas Kane later served in the United States Army as a major general during the Civil War, seeing action in the battles of Gettysburg and Chancelorsville. During his first visit with the Saints, Kane had requested and received a patriarchal blessing at the hands of Patriarch John Smith. He was promised, "Not a hair of your head will fall by the hand of an enemy. For you are called to do a great work on the earth and you shall be blessed in all your undertakings. Your name shall be had in honorable remembrance among the Saints to all generations" (quoted in Leonard J. Arrington, "'In Honorable Remembrance': Thomas L. Kane's Services to the Mormons," *BYU Studies* 21, no. 4 [Fall 1981], 393).

Fort Bridger

Established in 1843 by mountainmen Jim Bridger and Louis Vasquez, Fort Bridger served as a vital supply outpost to wagon trains traveling west on the Oregon, California, and Mormon trails. In 1852, a few years after the Saints settled the Salt Lake Valley, tensions between the Church and Jim Bridger began to rise after Bridger was accused of selling alcohol and weapons to local Native Americans, exacerbating the delicate conditions that existed between the Saints and their native neighbors. An arrest warrant was issued, and a group of Mormon militia was sent to arrest Bridger for his actions. Rather than face a confrontation with the Militia, Bridger left the fort and traveled east. A few years later, he agreed to sell the fort to the Church for eight thousand dollars.

The fort continued to serve a vital role as a rest and resupply depot for traveling wagon trains. In 1857 it was burnt to the ground by Major Lot Smith's men to keep it out of the hands of the federal troops. In the burned-out remains of the fort, General Johnston organized Camp Scott, where he and his men wintered before entering the Salt Lake Valley. While largely abandoned during the Civil War, the fort was taken over as a federal outpost for several decades after the war, only to be abandoned again in the late 1880s. It quickly fell into ruin and was sold in the early 1900s to the state of Wyoming to be restored as a state park.

September to November 1857

On August 29, 1857, President Buchanan appointed Colonel Albert Sidney Johnston as commander of the army en route for Utah, replacing Harney, who remained in Kansas.[27] Johnston immediately traveled west, arriving at Fort Leavenworth by the second week of September. There he assigned an escort of forty dragoons to accompany him on a hasty march to overtake his disorganized, brigade-size command. He also met newly appointed territorial governor Alfred Cumming of Georgia and the governor's entourage, consisting of his wife, several new federal judges, and others. Meanwhile, Lieutenant Colonel Philip St. George Cooke, commanding the Second Dragoons, was reorganizing and outfitting several companies of his regiment for the march to Utah. Cooke would lead his regiment and escort the governor and his party across the sparse high desert of Wyoming through a dreadful early winter season.

The story of the army's march to Utah serves as an example of a poorly led and organized campaign and of the misuse and loss of precious government property. Nonetheless, the march was supported by the skilled discipline and selfless service of American soldiers. Before Colonel Johnston arrived at Ham's Fork in western Wyoming, the Utah expedition was a spread-out and disorganized column, vulnerable to attack—and an attack is exactly what happened. For weeks, Mormon militia had hovered near the various infantry units and wagon trains. Then in early October, three of the army's wagon trains went up in smoke and hundreds of head of livestock were scattered. This severely hurt the expedition's logistical support, thus forcing Johnston to establish winter quarters near Fort Bridger, which the Saints had burned.[28]

The soldiers suffered through the winter, but Johnston imposed a strong arm of discipline, along with modest recreational diversions. Meanwhile, Mormon soldiers guarded the main entrance to the Great Basin at Echo Canyon.[29] Eventually, most of the men went home, leaving only a small detachment to watch the federal army.

During the winter, Thomas Kane, a non-Mormon military officer who was popular among the Saints, acted as an unofficial emissary from Buchanan to resolve the impasse. Through careful negotiation during months of crisis, war was averted and Governor Cumming was promised acceptance in Utah. At the same time, Lazarus W. Powell and Ben McCulloch arrived at Camp Scott as presidentially appointed commissioners to establish peace and federal authority.[30] General Scott had ordered reinforcements of another two thousand troops to Utah. Johnston was appointed commander of the new Department of Utah and received a brevet (honorary) promotion to brigadier general.

Brigham Young and other Church authorities declared that the Saints were never in rebellion. In return, they obtained a pardon for the destruction of government property and interference with military operations. With summer at hand, Johnston marched unmolested through Echo Canyon into Salt Lake City and continued south approximately thirty miles, where he established Camp Floyd, later renamed Fort Crittenden.[31] While some have suggested the poorly equipped and untrained Nauvoo Legion could have stopped the army at Echo Canyon, militarily speaking, such a possibility seems highly unlikely. With artillery that could have easily dislodged the Mormon defenses, Johnston would have been able to force his way through the canyon with minimal casualties.

Impact on Utah and the Church

With Cumming installed, the army garrisoned in Cedar Valley, and economic and judicial aspects restored, the Utah War ended. Nearly all results of the Utah War were regrettable. Brigham Young was replaced as territorial governor; more Gentiles (even undesired camp followers) and thousands of soldiers entered and occupied Utah; unwanted businesses, newspapers, drunkenness, and prostitution flourished; and additional federal officials, especially judges, were determined to indict and punish Mormons for crimes that included, most prominently, the Mountain Meadows Massacre. Yet not all results of the fray were negative. As a result of the conflict, Utah became open to more commerce and eventually joined the ranks of mainstream America.

After the Utah War, Mormon Zion was never the same. The Church lost the isolation it so desperately desired. Through more federal involvement and laws, officials and others were determined to undermine Church control and power. Yet in the long run, the Latter-day Saints succeeded. This commenced a struggle that lasted until polygamy was abolished in 1890 and statehood was granted in 1896. Through it all, the Church continued to prosper, erect temples, establish strong doctrinal and social foundations, and bring additional converts to Utah.

Notes

1. See Will Bagley, *Blood of the Prophets: Brigham Young and the Massacre at Mountain Meadows* (Norman, OK: University of Oklahoma Press, 2002); and Juanita Brooks, *The Mountain Meadows Massacre* (Norman, OK: University of Oklahoma Press, 1950).

2. See Robert W. Coakley, *The Role of Federal Military Forces in Domestic Disorders, 1789–1878* (Washington DC: U.S. Army Center of Military History, 1988).

3. Coakley, *The Role of Federal Military Forces*, 4–7, 24–35.

4. Norman F. Furniss, *The Mormon Conflict*, 1850–59 (New Haven: Yale University Press, 1960) 193.

5. See Furniss, *The Mormon Conflict*, 28.

6. Marcy's adventure is told in his autobiography (see Randolph Barnes Marcy, *Thirty Years of Army Life on the Border* [New York: Harper Brothers, 1866]).

7. Gregory J. W. Urwin, *The United States Cavalry: An Illustrated History* (New York: Blandford Press, 1985), 105.

8. See Donald R. Moorman with Gene A. Sessions, *Camp Floyd and the Mormons: The Utah War* (Salt Lake City: University of Utah Press, 1992), 6.

9. Bagley, *Blood of the Prophets*, has an entire chapter that deals with the Indian involvement with the Mormons against the federal army.

10. Furniss, *The Mormon Conflict*, 11.

11. Bagley, *Blood of the Prophets*, 22.

12. Coakley, *The Role of Federal Military Forces in Domestic Disorders*, 195.

13. Leonard J. Arrington, *Brigham Young: American Moses* (New York: Knopf, 1985), 223.

14. Coakley, *The Role of Federal Military Forces in Domestic Disorders*, 196.

15. Moorman, *Camp Floyd and the Mormons*, 273.

16. Bagley, *Blood of the Prophets*, 79.

17. LeRoy Hafen, *The Utah Expedition* (Glendale, CA: Arthur H. Clark and Company, 1958), 31.

18. William P. MacKinnon, "The Buchanan Spoils System and the Utah Expedition: Careers of W. M. F. Magraw and John M. Hockaday," *Utah Historical Quarterly* 31, no. 2 (Spring 1963): 144–45.

19. See Furniss, *The Mormon Conflict*, 123.

20. See Brooks, *The Mountain Meadows Massacre*, 35.

21. See Brooks, *The Mountain Meadows Massacre*, 19–21.

22. Furniss, *The Mormon Conflict*, 15–16.

23. See Furniss, *The Mormon Conflict*, 95.

24. See Furniss, *The Mormon Conflict*, 95.

25. See Furniss, *The Mormon Conflict*, 106.

26. See Furniss, *The Mormon Conflict*, 106.

27. See Furniss, *The Mormon Conflict*, 101.

28. See Hafen, *Utah Expedition*, 70–71; Coakley, *The Role of Federal Military Forces in Domestic Disorders*, 204.

29. See Furniss, *The Mormon Conflict*, 113.

30. See Furniss, *The Mormon Conflict*, 193.

31. Camp Floyd was established in November 1857, and by the summer of 1861 it was abandoned. Originally named for Secretary of War John B. Floyd, the camp was later renamed for Secretary of War John J. Crittenden after Floyd defected to the Confederate South at the time of the outbreak of war.

Introduction to the Civil War

> "WE FAILED, BUT IN THE GOOD PROVIDENCE OF GOD APPARENT FAILURE OFTEN PROVES A BLESSING."
> —*Robert E. Lee*

★ ★ ★

THE CIVIL WAR WAS A COMPLEX conflict that took this nation through its darkest period. The complexity of the Civil War involved every facet of life. The war tore at the heart of all that America stands for. It cut to the very core of the political, economic, and social elements of American life. The argument centered on where ultimate sovereignty lay—whether with the Union or with the individual states. It questioned the economic and social structure basis in slave power and agriculture in the South. The Civil War is remembered as the war that pitted brother against brother because of the brutal nature of the tensions at work.

In the words of then Secretary of State William H. Seward, the Civil War was the "irrepressible conflict." It has also been deemed an unnecessary bloodletting brought on by arrogant extremists and blundering politicians. Regardless of opinions, in 1861 the nation faced the very real prospect of a war that could dissolve the union.

Causes of the war were many and had developed over decades, but the immediate spark for the conflict came in consequence of South Carolina's determination to secede from the Union—a result of Abraham Lincoln's victory in the 1860 presidential election. South Carolina leaders had been waiting for an event to unite the South against antislavery forces. At a special convention called in South Carolina, a declaration was passed declaring that the United States of America was dissolved.

> **Causes of the war were many and had developed over decades.**

By February 1861, six Southern states had joined South Carolina in seceding. A provisional constitution for the Confederate States of America was adopted that month. The remaining Southern states continued residence with the Union. Less than a month later, on March 4, 1861, Abraham Lincoln was sworn in as president of the United States. In Lincoln's inaugural address, he refused to recognize the secession; he considered it legally void. He concluded his speech with a plea for restoration of the Union. However, in the South, Lincoln's plea fell on deaf ears. On April 12, the fighting began when Confederate forces fired on federal troops stationed at Fort Sumter in the Charleston harbor.

As a result, Union troops marched under the command of Major General Irvin McDowell toward the Confederate forces at Manassas, Virginia. The Union was blocked, and the First Battle of Bull Run ensued. The Confederate troops, under the command of General Joseph E. Johnston and Pierre G. T. Beauregard, forced Union troops back to Washington DC. Startled at the loss, and in an attempt to prevent the remaining slave states from leaving the Union, the United States Congress passed the Crittenden-Johnson Resolution on July 25, 1861. It declared that the war was being fought to preserve the Union, not to end slavery.

The war began in earnest in 1862. General Ulysses S. Grant brought the Union its first victory; he captured Fort Henry, Tennessee, on February 6 of that year. However, this victory was short lived. Major General George McClellan, of the Union, reached the gates of Richmond in the spring of 1862 only to be defeated by General Robert E. Lee in the Seven Days' Campaign. After this defeat, McClellan was relieved of command. His successor, John Pope, suffered the same fate when Lee beat him at the Second Battle of Bull Run in August.

Encouraged by Lee's success, the Confederacy invaded the North for the first time. General Lee led fifty-five thousand men of the Army of Northern Virginia across the Potomac into Maryland on September 5. Lincoln then reinstated McClellan, who won a bloody victory at the Battle of Antietam near Sharpsburg, Maryland, on September 17, 1862. Defeated, Lee's army returned to Virginia.

When McClellan failed to follow up on Antietam, Lincoln once again found a replacement: Major General Ambrose Burnside. Burnside suffered a near-immediate defeat at the Battle of Fredericksburg and was replaced by Major General Joseph Hooker. Hooker also proved insufficient to Lee's army and was replaced after the loss of the Battle of Chancellorsville in May 1863.

Lincoln found an able replacement in Major General George Meade, who stopped Lee's invasion of Union-held territory at the Battle of Gettysburg (July 1–3, 1863). General Lee's army suffered twenty-eight thousand casualties and was forced to retreat again to Virginia.

While the Confederate forces had some success in the eastern theater—holding on to their capital—the west was their downfall. Confederate forces were driven from Missouri early in the war, which allowed the Union to maintain possession of that key strategic state.

Nashville, Tennessee, fell to the Union early in 1862. The Mississippi River was opened to Vicksburg and then to Memphis. New Orleans was also captured early in 1862, allowing the Union forces to begin moving up the Mississippi.

The Union's strength increased with the strategic mind of Ulysses S. Grant. His gift was proven with the victories of Fort Donelson; the Battle of Shiloh; Vicksburg, Mississippi; and Chattanooga, Tennessee, where he drove Confederate forces out of Tennessee. Grant understood the concept of total war and realized, along with Lincoln, that only the utter defeat of Confederate forces would bring an end to the war. Grant was given command of all Union armies in 1864.

Union forces in the East attempted to maneuver past Lee and fought several battles during that phase of the eastern campaign: the Battle of the Wilderness, Spotsylvania, and Cold Harbor. An attempt to outflank Lee from the South failed under Generals Benjamin F. Butler and William F. Smith, who were contained in the Bermuda Hundred, a neck of land near the James and Appomattox rivers.

General Grant relentlessly pressed the Army of Northern Virginia under the command of General Lee. Grant pinned the Confederate army in the Siege of Petersburg and, after two failed attempts (under Siegel and Hunter), finally found an able commander,

Philip H. Sheridan, who could clear the threat to Washington DC from the Shenandoah Valley.

Meanwhile, Union general William Tecumseh Sherman marched from Chattanooga to the sea at Savannah, leaving nothing in his wake but destruction and ashes. He stuck to his statement that he gave shortly before beginning his brutal march: "War is cruelty. There is no use trying to reform it. The crueler it is, the sooner it will be over." When Sherman turned north through South and North Carolina to approach the Virginia lines from the south, it was the end for Lee and the Confederacy.

With Lee's surrender on April 9, 1865, at Appomattox Courthouse, the Union formally became the victor in the conflict. The last land battle of the war, the Battle of Palmito Ranch, was fought on May 13, 1865, in the far south of Texas and ended with a Confederate victory. However, the victory was meaningless because of Lee's surrender. All Confederate land forces surrendered by June 1865. Confederate naval units surrendered in November of 1865.

Despite the end of the war, conflict still existed. The post-war Reconstruction Era, headed by Grant, who was eventually elected president, would confront many obstacles, including persistent Southern resistance. Illustrative of the resistance were the "Jim Crow" laws, which essentially legalized racial discrimination. Decades of struggle followed, leading to an appeal for equality and unity in the nation. In a sense, the struggle for "one nation under God" has never ceased.

4

The Church and the Civil War

DAVID F. BOONE

★ ★ ★

IN THE ANNALS OF AMERICAN HISTORY, the Civil War stands unique. This horrific war is regarded as the most violent in American history. It is remembered as the most devastating conflict, measured in terms of economic cost and loss of American lives, and as the most tragic example of man's inhumanity to man. In terms of lives lost, the Civil War was more costly than all other American wars combined, with the exception of World War II. From the Church perspective,

David F. Boone is an associate professor of Church history and doctrine at Brigham Young University.

it was not the first war to involve Latter-day Saints, but it was the first formal conflict in which a Latter-day Saint died in battle.¹

In addition, over three hundred thousand were wounded in the terrible conflict. Whole communities were leveled by the armies of the North and of the South, sometimes more than once. Even after the guns were silenced, the deep wounds of the war took decades to heal during the reconstruction period and beyond. While visiting the famed battlefields of Bull Run, Shiloh, Gettysburg, or countless

Flag of the Eighth Pennsylvania Infantry. Courtesy of National Archives.

other fields of sorrow, it is hard to imagine the violence that divided the nation. Out of the tragic event, the nation was strengthened and finally made indivisible.

The Civil War also had a significant impact on Latter-day Saints even though they were geographically separated from the war-related devastation, having moved to the West. The Civil War battle closest to the Saints was most likely Picacho Peak in Arizona, which resulted in few deaths but resulted in a significant withdrawal of both Union and Confederate troops from the West to the eastern battlegrounds. No Latter-day Saints are known to have participated in this battle.

Church leaders suggested that moving West was in part a protection for the Church against the ravages of war. President Brigham Young noted, "The whispering of the Spirit to us have invariably been . . . to depart, to go hence, to flee into the mountains . . . that we may be secure in the visitation of the Judgments that must pass upon this land . . . while the guilty land of our fathers is purifying by the overwhelming scourge."[2]

Prophecy on War

As horrific as the Civil War was, the conflict was not unexpected for Latter-day Saints. Many years earlier, in 1832, Joseph Smith received a revelation titled a "Prophecy on War" (D&C 87). Received on Christmas Day,

A War Like No Other

No war can compare to the violence of the Civil War. The United States was not yet one hundred years old before it was nearly torn apart by the tragic conflict. It was a war in which father was pitted against son and brother against brother. The conflict between the North and the South resulted in more American casualties than all other American wars combined, before or since, with the exception of World War II. The death toll for the war is as follows:

Union forces
    Battle deaths: 140,414
    Other deaths: 224,097

Confederate forces
    Battle deaths: 74,524
    Other deaths: 59,297

(www.infoplease.com/ipaA0004615.html; accessed October 18, 2006)

the revelation foretold an unparalleled conflict—one that would envelop not only the entire nation but other nations as well. Some recognized that there was a crisis in South Carolina in November 1832, but it did not escalate into war. On April 2, 1843, Joseph Smith received another revelation on the same subject. This revelation stands today as Doctrine and Covenants 130. It also predicted that the conflict would commence in South Carolina but provided further insight, saying, "It may probably arise through the slave question" (D&C 130:13).

The American Civil War was approximately twenty-nine years away when the first revelation on war, which would become Doctrine and Covenants 87, was given and eighteen years away when the second revelation, Doctrine and Covenants 130, was given. Both revelations were published years before the predicted events began to unfold. In 1851, Elder Franklin D. Richards first published the 1832 revelation (D&C 87) in the inaugural edition of the Pearl of Great Price. Three years later, the revelation was published again in *The Seer*. Missionaries carried copies of the revelations and read them as a part of their preaching. In a discourse delivered in the Tabernacle in Salt Lake City on January 1, 1871, Wilford Woodruff recalled that he wrote down the revelation that would become Doctrine and Covenants 87 for his own use "twenty-five years before the rebellion took place; others also wrote it, and it was published to the world before there was any prospect of the fearful events it predicted coming to pass."[3]

Elder Jedediah M. Grant read the revelation from the courthouse steps in Tazewell County, Virginia, during one of his early missionary journeys to the Burkes Garden area, where he enjoyed remarkable success. The revelation was also read and taught by missionaries in South Carolina in 1838–39.[4] Elder Grant often used the prophecy during his proselyting efforts in the Southern states.[5]

Other leaders spoke in a similar spirit of prophecy. In Paris, Tennessee, in the face of threats of mob violence, Elder David W.

Brother Joseph ©1998 David Lindsley. Courtesy of IRI.

Patten prophesied in a manner similar to the war revelations of Joseph Smith. The following was said about his predictions: "Instead . . . of being intimidated . . . David denounced their undertaking in the most unmeasured terms and in the spirit of prophecy . . .

predicted: 'Before you die some of you will see the streets of [Paris, Tennessee] run with the blood of its own citizens.'" Years later, Patten's biographer noted, "How fearfully this prophecy was fulfilled in the capture of [Paris, Tennessee] in 1862 by General [John Hunt] Morgan [Confederate general], during his famous raid through Kentucky and Tennessee!"6

Numerous additional statements were made concerning the impending conflict, which was believed to have been brought on by the wickedness of the nations and the ill treatment of the Saints from New York to Illinois. For example, Wilford Woodruff remembered the Prophet Joseph explaining, when asked when these things would be, "that whosoever lived to see the two sixes come together in '66 would see the American continent deluged in blood."7

Two days prior to the Prophet's martyrdom in Carthage Jail, the Prophet spoke to a group of his antagonists. He told them that they thirsted for his blood. He prophesied, "You shall witness scenes of blood and sorrow to your entire satisfaction. Your souls shall be perfectly satiated with blood, . . . and those people that desire this great evil upon me and my brethren, shall be filled with regret and sorrow because of the scenes of desolation and distress that await them." He also told them that "many of you who are now present shall have an opportunity to face the cannon's mouth from sources you think not of."8 It has been suggested that the Civil War lasted twice as long in Missouri as it did anywhere else because of the border conflicts, the guerrillas, and the general mayhem that devastated the state for almost half a century following the actual war.

After the war, in a discourse dated August 1876, Elder Orson Pratt remembered, "When I was a boy I traveled extensively in the United States and the Canadas, preaching this restored gospel. I had a manuscript copy of this revelation [D&C 87], which I carried in my pocket, and I was in the habit of reading it to the people among whom I traveled and preached." Like Elder Grant, "the people regarded it as the height of nonsense, saying the Union was too strong to be broken. . . . [But] I knew the prophecy was true. . . . This is another testimony that Joseph Smith was a prophet of the Most High God."⁹

Some details of the revelation were so specific that they could only refer to the Civil War and were unmistakably fulfilled.¹⁰ The prophecy indicated that war would "shortly come to pass, beginning at the rebellion of South Carolina" (D&C 87:1). The Civil War began on April 12, 1861, when Confederate troops under General Pierre G. T. Beauregard fired on Fort Sumter in South Carolina. Joseph Smith also prophesied that the war would "eventually terminate in the death and misery of many souls" (v. 1), and that "war will be poured out upon all nations, beginning at this place" (v. 2). Many fail to realize that the events in this prophecy, beginning with the Civil War, have come to pass and are continuing to be fulfilled. The Lord furthered revealed, "Southern States shall be divided against the Northern States" (v. 3). "The Southern States will call on other nations . . . in order

The Civil War in Missouri

The Civil War in Missouri essentially began in 1854. Missouri was a key state to both Northern and Southern politicians. It was divided nearly equally between pro- and antislavery advocates. More importantly, Missouri was one of the strongest of the frontier territories. So in 1854, when Kansas voted to choose a territorial legislature, proslavery groups in Missour organized their followers and crossed the border en masse to ensure that a proslavery legislature was elected. Their tactic worked, yet antislavery groups raised many questions when they discovered that in the election, over six thousand votes had been cast when the territory had barely registered three thousand voters. Tensions between these two groups escalated to border raids and skirmishes between the proslavery "Ruffians" from Missouri and the antislavery "Jayhawkers" from Kansas, leading to what was known as "Bleeding Kansas."

When war broke out in 1861, Missourians voted to remain with the Union. The Missouri governor, a proslavery advocate, protested the vote and established a rebel government, essentially in exile. Government armories were seized and soon full-scale battles erupted in the state. By 1865 over 1,100 engagements had been fought on Missouri soil, second only to the state of Virginia, and tens of thousands of soldiers had died. Missouri also provided 60 percent of its adult male population (over 150,000) to the armies of the North and South.

to defend themselves" and named specifically Great Britain (v. 3). Both of these came to pass and are well documented in the history of the Civil War.

Finally, the revelation foretold that "slaves shall rise up against their masters, who shall be marshaled and disciplined for war" (v. 4). Since the Civil War was, in part, fought over the institution of slavery, and since the Emancipation Proclamation began the process of freeing slaves and abolishing slavery, former slaves were able to take up arms in the conflict. This is likewise consistent with the teachings of the Prophet Joseph Smith: "It is not right that any man should be in bondage one to another" (D&C 101:79).[11]

Latter-day Saint Expectations of the Coming Conflict

Before the outbreak of war in April 1861, a number of Latter-day Saints resided in the East. Some were converts who had lagged behind the Saints that had already immigrated West, and some were on their way to join the Saints in the West. Few missionaries would have been a part of the Eastern population of Saints at the time since most had returned to the West at the outset of the Utah War. Most of the converts were from New England, New York, and other Northern states. The first Latter-day Saint converts in the South were baptized in 1831. Some areas, such as South Carolina, did not record convert baptisms until the late 1830s.[12] While their numbers were sparse, nonetheless, these Latter-day Saints were obviously affected by the war. Indeed, Church members were involved on both sides of the conflict.[13]

A few Latter-day Saint converts who emigrated from Europe to gather with their fellow Saints found it advisable to join the war effort in order to secure additional funds to continue the long journey to the West. These converts joined both sides of the war effort, ostensibly because they were arriving at ports where recruitment was available. There were many ports of entry in the Northeast and some ports in the South.¹⁴

John Davis Evans was a Latter-day Saint who immigrated to the United States during this period. Evans was born on March 4, 1843, in Hirwain, South Wales, and was baptized at the age of seven. Shortly after his family's conversion, Evans's father, Daniel Evans, was called to be president of a branch of the Church in South Wales. Desiring to gather with the Saints in America, Daniel Evans and his family left Liverpool, England, aboard the ship *Joseph Badger* on October 7, 1850. Nearly six weeks later, the Evans family arrived at the port of New Orleans. They soon moved to St. Louis, Missouri, where Daniel Evans secured work in a coal mine. It was during this employment that he was crushed to death by a large chunk of coal.¹⁵

In 1859, John Davis Evans joined with a company of Latter-day Saints at Florence, Nebraska, and made the journey to the Salt Lake Valley, arriving on September 1, 1859. He was later responsible for driving a team of oxen across the plains on three separate occasions to help other pioneers make their way to the Salt Lake Valley.¹⁶

On June 1, 1861, John Davis Evans enlisted as a private in Company D of the 7th Missouri Volunteer Infantry Regiment, which was subsequently accepted into the

Evans Union Ice Cream Company

After the Civil War, John Davis Evans returned to the Salt Lake Valley to make a home. He married Margaret Williams in the Endowment House on July 16, 1870. The Evans family settled in St. John, Tooele County, Utah, where Evans first worked in the canyons collecting cedar posts that he burned to make charcoal, which he then sold in Salt Lake City. Hardworking and industrious, Evans helped lay the first train tracks into Pleasant Valley. Evans worked as a teamster hauling salt from the salt beds around Great Salt Lake and also hauled granite from the canyon for the Salt Lake Temple. Around 1890, Evans and his wife started one of the first ice cream companies in Salt Lake City, which they called "Evans Union Ice Cream." The patriotism of the Evans family was evident in the company name and logo. The logo for the Evans Union Ice Cream company was a red, white, and blue shield, which hung on the side of the company wagon that traveled the streets of Salt Lake City. John Davis Evans passed away on July 30, 1908, at the age of sixty-six (John Davis Evans Papers, courtesy of the Evans family).

96th Pennsylvania Infantry at Camp Northumberland near Washington DC, circa 1861. Courtesy of National Archives.

Union Army. Research done by Evans's daughter revealed that "he [Evans] was the only man from Utah to return to his own state to enlist."[17]

In May of 1862, Evans and the 7th Missouri Infantry arrived at Pittsburg Landing, Tennessee. Pittsburg Landing was the site for the Battle of Shiloh, where the Union had been victorious just several weeks before. General Albert Sidney Johnston led the Confederate forces at Shiloh and was killed in battle while fighting against federal authority over the South. This was the same Johnston who, in 1858, commanded the federal troops that marched into Salt Lake City to exert federal control over Utah Territory.[18] Evans and the 7th Missouri saw varying degrees of action throughout the Civil

War. However, their principle mission was silencing the guns at Vicksburg.

William Rex is another Latter-day Saint whose story of involvement in the war is compelling. As an English convert, Rex came to the States with his family in 1850 and established a home in St. Louis, Missouri. Misfortune visited the family in 1852 when William's father died, leaving a widow and several young children. To earn a living, William and his brothers would swim the Mississippi River in search of drifting logs to sell to neighbors. At age seventeen, William left home near the end of the war to join the Union Army. The certificate of his enlistment required his service for 110 days. During this time he served in the campaign of General Sherman and participated in victories over the South in Georgia.

After the war, Rex made his way to Utah in 1869 along with his mother and brother Alfred on the first trainload of cattle to go West on the new railroad. William went on to contribute greatly to the Church, to his family, and to the community of Randolph, Utah, where he eventually settled.[19]

Abraham Lincoln and the Latter-day Saints

As early as the 1840s, Abraham Lincoln was familiar with the Latter-day Saints. Prior to being an Illinois Congressman and before his ascent to the American presidency, Lincoln voted for the Nauvoo Charter in 1840, which essentially authorized the City of Nauvoo to have a fully autonomous local government.[20] While it is not known whether Abraham Lincoln and Joseph Smith ever met face to face, evidence suggests that they may have, and it is likely that each was acquainted with the other's political inclinations. They were both in Springfield, Illinois, at the same time on several occasions, and evidence suggests that the two leaders had mutual friends.[21] President Heber J. Grant once said, "I believe that Lincoln was acquainted

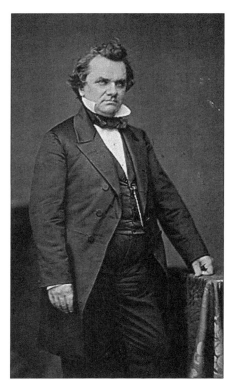

Senator Stephen A. Douglas, circa 1856. Courtesy of Church Archives.

with the Prophet Joseph Smith, at any rate that he [Lincoln] knew of our drivings and persecutions in New York, Ohio, and Missouri, before we located in Nauvoo."[22] As for Lincoln's understanding of Latter-day Saints, records indicate that in 1861–62 the president checked out several books from the Library of Congress on Mormonism, including the Book of Mormon.[23]

One politician who was a mutual acquaintance of both Lincoln and the Mormons was Illinois senator Stephen A. Douglas. Douglas is remembered for his participation in the debates in 1858 as he and Lincoln actively pursued the presidency of the United States. Previously, Douglas served as the secretary of state for Illinois, where he "enrolled the [newly passed] Nauvoo Charter in the official archives of Illinois."[24] Later, while acting as a judge, Douglas was a dinner guest with the Prophet Joseph in the home of Jacob Backenstos in Carthage, where the Prophet is said to have prophesied that Douglas's political success was contingent upon his support of the Latter-day Saints. Joseph prophesied: "Judge, you will aspire to the presidency of the United States; and if ever you turn your hand against me or the Latter-day Saints, you will feel the weight of the hand of the Almighty upon you." Judge Douglas, the record states, "appeared very friendly," and the Prophet Joseph concluded, "You will live to see and know that I have testified the truth to you; for the conversation of this day will stick to you through life."²⁵ Later, Douglas publicly turned against the Church, and he lived to see his political ambitions destroyed.²⁶ Douglas died less than a year after he lost the bid for the presidency.

Eruption of War

Whatever President Lincoln's early opinion toward the Latter-day Saints had been, his view of the Mormons seems to have mellowed once his presidency began. As President Lincoln became acquainted with his office, he became an expert at judging who could be trusted. President Young sent Congressional Representative William Hooper and others to confer with the president on territorial matters. It appears that the president was able to separate the rhetoric of biased individuals from those who more honestly represented the Church and its position. Finally, the president may have determined to avoid some of the misunderstandings and poor choices of previous administrations, most notably that of his immediate predecessor, James Buchanan.

Once war erupted in April 1861, Lincoln's time was fully consumed by the war, which lasted longer and impacted the nation

President Abraham Lincoln, 1864.
Courtesy of National Archives.

much more than initially expected, thus pushing other issues into the background. Even if Lincoln had the disposition to suppress the Latter-day Saints in the West, he did not have the funding, military resources, or manpower to do so. Perhaps influenced by his previous involvement with issues regarding the Saints, he adopted a policy of avoidance. When T. B. H. Stenhouse asked Lincoln what policy he would pursue with regard to the Mormons, Lincoln said, "Stenhouse, when I was a boy on the farm in Illinois there was a great deal of timber on the land which we had to clear away. Occasionally we would come to a log which had fallen down. It was too hard to split, too wet to burn and too heavy to move, so we plowed around it. That's what I intend to do with the Mormons. You go back [to Utah] and tell Brigham Young that if he will let me alone, I will let him alone."[27]

North-South Sentiments in Utah

In general conference, April 6, 1861, only days before the outbreak of the Civil War at Fort Sumter, President Brigham Young noted, "The whole Government is gone; it is as weak as water. I heard Joseph Smith say, nearly thirty years ago, 'They shall have mobbing to their heart's content, if they do not redress the wrongs of the Latter-day Saints.'"[28] In this same general conference, John Taylor spoke on what the Saints ought to do during the war between the North and South. Taylor declared, "What shall we do in the midst of these things that are now transpiring? Why, lean upon the Lord our God, purify ourselves. . . . Let us also look at our position as Elders in Israel, clothed with the power of the holy Priesthood, as men who hold the ministry of reconciliation. . . . This is the position that we ought to occupy in relation to these matters."[29] At a Fourth of July celebration almost three months later, Elder John Taylor further commented, "It may now be proper to inquire what part shall we take in the present difficulties. . . . We have neither inaugurated it,

President Brigham Young, circa 1870. © by Intellectual Reserve, Inc.

nor assisted in its inauguration. . . . Shall we join the North to fight against the South? No! Shall we join the south against the north? As emphatically, No! Why? They have both. . . . brought it upon themselves, and we have had no hand in the matter. . . . We know no north, no south, no east, no west."[30]

Midway through the war, in October of 1863, Brigham Young summarized his view of the parties of the ongoing conflict:

> I care for the North and the South and if I had sufficient power with the Lord, I would save every innocent man, woman and child from being slaughtered in this unnatural and almost universal destruction of life and property. . . . I care for the North and South more than I do for gold, and I would do a great deal, if I had the power, to ameliorate the condition of suffering thousands. I care enough for them to pray that righteous men may hold the reins of government, and that wicked, tyrannical despotism may be wiped away from the land.[31]

Despite occasional statements of Church leaders counseling against overtly allying with either side in the conflict, some Church members found themselves sympathizing with one side or the other. Most Church members were from states united with the Union. Still, there were the Southern sympathizers. Most of the feelings generated for the South came from areas where there was a concentration of Latter-day Saints who had joined the Church south of the Mason-Dixon Line. Such concentrated populations resulted from the Church practice of organizing communities according to residents' culture and geographic background.

In 1857, President Young determined that cotton should be grown in southern Utah. Washington County was chosen as the place, and converts from Texas and other Southern states who had experience raising cotton were among those initially called. This mission may have been a precaution against war or simply an effort to develop natural resources.

During the war years, Washington County produced a huge surplus of cotton. The extra seventy thousand pounds of cotton not needed in Church settlements was exported to markets along the Mississippi River. The production of cotton in Utah was a huge blessing to the Church during the Civil War because the supply of Southern cotton was cut off and was either used exclusively for the South's own needs or was exported to British and European ports, where it could be sold for top dollar.

Calling Southern pioneers from all over Utah Territory to Washington County to participate in the cotton-growing venture also brought a concentration of individuals from the South with common backgrounds.[32] These Southern converts shared a sympathy for their previous homeland and the causes that drew the South into the war. Sympathetic reactions in Utah for the South were isolated. The only recorded organized effort came from Washington County. It was viewed as significant enough that a General Authority was dispatched to resolve the matter.

The excitement surrounding this incident was caused by Colonel Benjamin Davies, a non–Latter-day Saint. Davies came to Utah in December 1860 as a federal appointee to serve as superintendent of Indian Affairs. He was in Utah when hostilities erupted in South Carolina in April 1861. As a Southerner himself, Davies assumed the role in Utah of recruiter for the Confederacy and was naturally drawn to the concentrations of Latter-day Saint Southerners in the area.

His rhetoric and passion for the Confederacy apparently caused some to reflect on their allegiances and reignited some feelings for the cause of defending their homeland. Church leaders were charged with visiting the communities to help the local Saints understand the precariousness of the Church's and Utah Territory's position relative to America and its Constitution, and the desire of the Church's leaders to gain acceptance within the United States. Few outward acts of loyalty to the Confederacy are noted, but occasionally individuals did voice their preferences.

Historian Chad Orton has noted a few minor and generally unrelated incidents involving Southern sympathizers in the West.[33]

David Harold Peery

Born in Tazewell County, Virginia on May 16, 1824, David was the son of Major David Peery and Eleanor Harmon. His father was a plantation and slave owner, and David worked alongside the slaves when not pursuing an education. As a young adult, he determined a preference for commerce rather than agriculture and became a store clerk. While in his store, he first met his future wife, a Latter-day Saint named Nancy Higginbotham. David and Nancy were married on December 30, 1852, and continued to reside and work in southwest Virginia, but he couldn't accept her religion. Frustrated at his inability to show her the error of her faith, he hired preachers to enlighten her, but she confounded them as well.

In 1862 David enlisted in the Confederate Army of Eastern Kentucky under General Humphrey Marshal but contracted typhoid fever and was returned to his father's home in a military ambulance. David lost his wife, two sons, both his parents, and his wife's father to the dreaded typhoid fever. While in deep mourning and combating illness, David began to think deeply about his own spiritual welfare and read the books Nancy had gathered about Mormonism. "Being much distressed in mind, I became greatly interested in the Gospel, reading the Bible and the writings of Parley and Orson Pratt. . . . [I] became convinced of the truth of the Latter-day work. One of the doctrines that particularly impressed me was marriage for eternity" (quoted in William G. Hartley, "The Confederate Officer and 'That Mormon Girl,'" *Ensign*, April 1982, 53). He rode twenty-five miles in extreme weather conditions to find Absalom Young, a Latter-day Saint elder, to baptize him. He was baptized on November 1863, having to dig through deep snow and cut through six inches of ice to access the water. Following baptism, he returned to the war, joining General John Stuart Williams's campaign in Kentucky, but he contracted typhoid fever once again. For over a month in 1864, David's life hung in the balance. David finally returned home again, only to find that Union troops had destroyed his home, store, and six warehouses.

With his discharge papers in hand, David joined his wife's mother, her children, and Leticia, his only surviving daughter, as they traveled west to join the Saints in Utah. Their early travel was assisted by a Confederate escort that accompanied them through areas of conflict. They traveled to Omaha, Nebraska, purchased wagons and livestock, and followed the pioneer trail to Salt Lake. In Utah he made a new start, marrying his wife's sister, Letitia. They had ten more children.

At the conclusion of the Civil War, he served a mission to his native Virginia and was called as stake president. He was twice elected mayor of Ogden and served for years as a delegate in the Utah Territorial legislature. On September 17, 1901, David died at his Ogden home, nicknamed "the Virginia," at age seventy-seven (Andrew Jenson, *LDS Biographical Encyclopedia* [Salt Lake City: Deseret News, 1901], 1:756).

One account described individuals in the Latter-day Saint Colorado settlements, where "it was not uncommon for Southern supporters to fly the Confederate flag." In a more emotionally charged incident, two individuals, presumably Southerners, voiced their position that "'Jeff Davis is a Gentleman and old Abe Lincoln is a son of a———.'" For their outburst the two men were put in chains and spent two days in confinement and "were released only after [they had sworn] an oath of allegiance to the United States and the local bishop warned that such language would not be tolerated in the future."[34]

It is unknown if any Southern Latter-day Saints left Utah to participate in the Civil War or if Davies had any success recruiting. A number of Latter-day Saints did, however, serve in the Civil War, but most of them joined from their home states before coming West. It is also known that Davies and a significant contingent of professional soldiers from Camp Floyd, including their superior officer, General Albert Sidney Johnston, left Utah's Camp Floyd and joined the Southern cause.[35]

As the war progressed, attitudes changed. Bravado and recklessness diminished on both sides as people were mollified and began regarding former enemies as fellowmen suffering under the indignities of war. Further, as the war progressed, and as awareness of the death and destruction of the war increased, the sharpness of the rhetoric seemed to ease on all fronts.

The Captain Robert F. Burton Company of Volunteers

On October 16, 1861, just six months after the war began, the overland telegraph line was completed to Salt Lake City. The nationwide telegraph literally connected the eastern and western shores of the continent together, which allowed the Saints in the Rocky Mountains to be connected with the rest of the nation.

President Young was given the honor of sending the first message across the wire, largely because of his emphasis on the project and because of Latter-day Saint support. President Young addressed the president of the telegraph company, congratulating him on his achievement and saying, "Utah has not seceded, but is firm for the Constitution and laws of our happy country, and is warmly interested in such useful enterprises as the one so far completed."[36]

On April 25 of the ensuing year, a telegram was sent from acting governor Frank Fuller to Daniel H. Wells, militia commander over the Utah Territory, requesting a company of volunteers "for military protection of mails, passengers, and the property of the mail company from the depredations of hostile Indians."[37] This company was to consist of "twenty mounted men duly officered and properly armed and equipped, carrying sufficient ammunition for thirty days' service in the field," and was to be commanded by Colonel Robert T. Burton. The company was also to be "furnished with the necessary commissary, stores and forage with proper means of transportation for the same."[38]

> "The men are very tired and wet. Having done today what the Mail Company could not do, and what they swore we could not."

Colonel Burton was to have full "discretion" and autonomy "as to the movements of his command," including the "term of service necessary to insure the safety and security of the mail and all persons and property connected therewith, and will communicate freely by telegraph" conditions that he encountered.[39] In addition to the twenty men called for, Burton selected men as teamsters to drive the wagons carrying the company's supplies. These teamsters did the work of privates in the U.S. Army. In addition to the protection of the mail routes, the company was further expected to escort territorial officials Chauncey W. West and William H. Hooper through Indian lands on their way to Washington DC.

Burton's volunteers left Salt Lake City on April 26, 1862, traveling east along the U.S. mail route. Due to poor weather, difficult traveling conditions, and delays getting supplies, their initial progress was slow. They passed through several mountain canyons still heavy with snowdrifts—experiencing deplorable traveling conditions. Burton documented his company's travel. He wrote, "We were three hours getting through a drift of snow . . . twenty rods long by as many feet deep . . . the men being in cold snow water most of the time. I never saw men work more freely, although the water was so cold that their legs would be perfectly numb." After the intense exertion, the men were exhausted. Burton reported, "The men are very tired and wet. Having done today what the Mail Company could not do, and what they swore we could not."[40]

At Fort Bridger, the mail company found reports of Indians attacking the mail stations and personnel, thereby justifying their being called into service. Burton reported, "Six men had been wounded, two of them severely, they were now in the hospital."[41] From then on, the evidence of further depredations continued and became more frequent.

Burton's volunteers subsequently reported visiting thirty mail stations between Salt Lake City and the Platte River Crossing. Of those stations visited, he noted, "All the stations this side of Green River look as though they had been deserted in a hurry."[42] The apparent reason for the hasty departure from the mail stations and an obvious reason for the appointment of the Latter-day Saint volunteers included depredations from marauding Native Americans who stampeded the livestock, scattered the mail, and destroyed government and individual property. Furthermore, Native Americans trashed and burned the mail stations, and attacked the mail employees, killing some.

Lot's One Hundred, painting by Frank Thomas. Courtesy of Frank Thomas.

Initially, the instigators of these attacks on government facilities were believed to be members of the Bannock and Snake tribes under the leadership of Chief Pashago. Additional evidence against them was provided by mail contractors who had fled for their lives. Burton, however, believed and noted evidence that some of the depredations were caused by American emigrants, including mountaineers, gold seekers, and other western travelers.

At one station along the Sweetwater River, Burton's men found a note that an earlier traveler posted to a telegraph pole. The note warned subsequent travelers, "We left here in a big hurry," and then suggested, "The depredations committed . . . were done by Mormons and Snake Indians."[43] When the accusors were confronted with their notes, they denied being involved, although some of their names were attached to the note.

As they traveled further eastward, Burton's company gathered mail and personal belongings and stored them for safekeeping until they or others could return to retrieve them. After reaching Devil's Gate on May 16, Hooper and West, with an escort of eight of Burton's men, including Brigham Young Jr., continued east on their journey.[44] Burton and the remainder of his company remained at

Devil's Gate awaiting further orders from Salt Lake City. They eventually started their return trip west to the Salt Lake Valley.

On Wednesday, May 21, after having commenced their return trip, Burton's Company encountered another military unit composed of Latter-day Saints. This second company, a group numerically superior to the one headed by Burton, was led by Lot Smith. Smith's unit possessed enough manpower to enable them to chase the marauding tribes and retrieve stolen livestock. They had conducted a military court that tried some of the Caucasian offenders. Burton's men gathered several dozen mail bags and delivered them to government mail agents who took them the remainder of the way east or west to their intended destinations. The delivery of the delayed mail was one early sign of the success of the company. Colonel Robert T. Burton and his remaining soldiers returned to Salt Lake City on Saturday evening, May 31, having exceeded their original expectation of military service by six days.

Lot Smith's Utah Volunteers

"On April 28, 1862, the Adjutant General of the Army, by express direction of President Lincoln telegraphed Brigham Young[45] of Salt Lake City, [providing] the authority to raise, arm, and equip [a] Company of Cavalry for 90 days' service."[46] The company was immediately organized and placed under the command of Captain Lot Smith. One hundred and five men were mustered into the service of the United States Army, and the organization became known as "Captain Lot Smith's Company of Utah Calvary." Their initial term of service was for ninety days with instructions "to protect the property of the telegraph and overland mail service, between Forts Bridger and Laramie, to continue in service until the United States troops shall reach the point where their services are needed."[47]

On April 30, 1862, the *Deseret News* reported, "The company will not, according to the specifications of the order, be required to perform any other service than that required for the protection of the mail and telegraph."[48] In their "official call," the company was assured that they "*will not be employed for any offensive operations other than may grow out of the duty herein assigned to it.*"[49] The Church acted quickly, desiring to be seen as supportive of the Union, the war effort, and the U.S. Constitution. Still, in both Burton and Smith's missions there seemed to be no likelihood of engaging the soldiers of the Southern rebellion. Within two days, the company was organized. The men were briefed on their assignments and then were given specific instruction. President Young and General Daniel H. Wells ate dinner with the company before they left the Salt Lake Valley, and both "gave them some excellent advice and counsel," including the importance of their assignment. President Young reminded them that their loyalty to the United States of America was their first and primary responsibility and "that they must defend the Union at all hazards, even to the sacrificing of their lives" if necessary.[50] They were reminded to remember their daily prayers, a practice that was observed as a camp each day they were in the service.

President Young further directed them, "I desire of the officers and privates of this company, that in this service they will conduct themselves as gentlemen, remembering their allegiance and loyalty to our government, and also not forgetting that they are members of the organization to which they belong." He cautioned them to never indulge in intoxicants of any kind and warned them against "associating with bad men or lewd women, always seeking to make peace with the Indians. Aim never to take the life of an Indian or white man, unless compelled to do so in the discharge of duty, or in defense of your own lives, or that of your comrades." Some of the volunteers in this company, including commander Lot Smith himself, had served in the Mormon Battalion and were also involved in the Utah War.

President Young concluded his counsel by instructing the men, "Another thing I would have you remember is that, although you are United States soldiers you are still members of the Church of Jesus Christ of Latter-day Saints, and while you have sworn allegiance to the constitution and government of our country, and we have vowed to preserve the Union, the best way to accomplish this high purpose," he said, "is to shun all evil . . . , remember your prayers, . . . establish peace with the Indians, . . . always give ready obedience to the orders of your commanding officers. If you do this," the President noted, "I promise you, as a servant of the Lord, that not one of you shall fall by the hand of an enemy."[51]

One of the militia members, Private Charles Crismon Jr., recorded an unusual piece of instruction to the departing recruits. Crismon remembered that after counseling the men to abstain from liquor and to avoid profanity, President Young said, "When you are offered the United States uniform, do not wear it." Crismon later noted, "We were given the Soldier's uniform . . . but still wore the clothing that we used when we equipped ourselves at Salt Lake City." Years later, Crismon met with some Washakie Indians who were by this time peaceful. Crismon related from his discussion with them, "At one time our men were totally surrounded by them in ambush. If they had thought we were U.S. soldiers and had seen us in the national uniform, we would have all been killed." The fact that they were obedient to this unusual counsel from their Prophet-leader and "wore the clothing of the 'Mormon' settlers, saved us."[52]

Lot Smith's company served with distinction, although their tour of duty was not easy. Harvey C. Hullinger, a private in the company, is the only member identified who kept a daily journal during his four months of service. Hullinger's record contains insights of his fellow soldiers and chronicles the hardships experienced by the troops. When the company left Salt Lake in late April, there was so much snow that the company determined to go up Emigration Canyon rather than Parley's Canyon. On "one occasion early in the march, they encountered ten feet of newly fallen snow," which made the roads nearly impassable.[53] The men had to build or rebuild bridges. When the snow melted, the torrential flow of water washed out bridges and roads. Hullinger noted, "The roads became muddier. . . . At times we had to fasten ropes to the horses and pull them out of the mud and help them up the hills. As we reached the summit, the road became almost impassable. It took us four hours to travel less than a mile."[54] Private Joseph A. Fisher remembered that "at one part of the journey he was without a dry stitch of clothing day or night for three weeks; his comrades suffered the same exposure with him."[55]

Lot Smith's company served under the direction of a regiment of Ohio Volunteers under the command of Colonel Collins. The colonel said to Captain Smith one day, "I would like to try a test and see whether your men or mine are best adapted to remain here in the West." The colonel then ordered a detachment of mounted Eastern soldiers to the top of a mountain. "They went up and came down in great confusion." Lot Smith's company, on the other hand, gave their horses their reins, "and the horses of themselves avoided the sage brush and gopher holes" since they were used to the terrain. Collins remarked to Lot as a result of his test of the men, "I would rather have ten of your men than my whole regiment. We will send the Eastern men [back] to the [battle's] front."[56]

Lot Smith's service was meritorious, both in the eyes of his military commanders and Church leaders. Both groups roundly praised the Utah Volunteers for their service. Still, Smith was viewed in the military hierarchy as a controversial figure since he had taken up arms against the federal government in the Utah War and by so doing was accused of being disloyal to the Union. President Brigham

Young's instruction to the Mormon raiders who were involved early in defending the homes of the Latter-day Saints in the Utah War was to "keep back the on-coming army of ten thousand men, and not shed one drop of blood." Consequently, "Lot Smith . . . did more to check the army and prevent its advance into [the] Salt Lake Valley . . . than any other man save it be Brigham Young, under whose orders he was acting." In Lot Smith's defense, "it has been said of him," Fisher noted, "that were it not for his unpopular religion he would have become one of the greatest generals of the Civil War."[57]

Following the Civil War, an investigation concluded that Smith's soldiers were indeed eligible for veteran's benefits. The investigation showed that "Lot Smith's Company of Utah Cavalry was duly mustered into the Military Service of the United States Army, . . . [had] served between April 12, 1861, and April 9, 1865, in the War for the suppression of the Rebellion, . . . [and were] honorably discharged" following their official service and were thereby "eligible for membership in the Grand Army of the Republic."[58]

Connor's California Volunteers

General Patrick Edward Connor was born in County Kerry, Ireland, and immigrated to New York City, where he was raised. He entered the regular U.S. Army as an enlisted man, saw early military action against the Seminole Indians in Florida, and later served as a captain in the Mexican War, where he was wounded in the battle of Buena Vista. The gold rush and the lure of mining drew Connor to California following the war with Mexico. There he reenlisted in the regular army just as the Civil War broke out in the East. Connor was sent to Utah as a colonel of the California Volunteers to protect the communication lines and trails between Wyoming and Nevada, much as Lot Smith and Robert T. Burton had done at the outset of the war. Utah historian Gustive O. Larson noted, "Utah's course of history was affected when the avowed enemy of the Saints [Connor], who had been assigned to protect the Overland Mail assumed also to watch and combat Mormonism."[59]

While in Utah, Connor became an antagonist toward the Latter-day Saints, spearheading efforts to break up the Church's influence through mining activities, which encouraged non-Mormons to move to the area. Only partially successful in his quest, Connor was nevertheless remembered as "the father of Utah Mining." He further established a newspaper in Salt Lake City, run by members of his military force, named the *Daily Union Vedette*, which for years was the non-Mormon voice in the territory and was sharply critical

> War is miserable for those who survive it, support it, or endure it. It is much harder for those who actually participate in it.

of the Latter-day Saints.[60]

Rather than establish his command at Camp Floyd, Connor took his men and established a permanent military post on the east bench, overlooking Salt Lake City. Apparently as an intentional affront to the Saints and against their expressed wishes, the encampment was named Camp Douglas after the Church's earlier friend-turned-antagonist Stephen A. Douglas.

From this vantage point, in close proximity to Church headquarters, Connor became a thorn in the side of Church leaders when friction erupted because of the abrasive demeanor and occasional lawless activities of many of Connor's men. After his tenure in the U.S. Army ended, Connor remained in the community, where he participated in everything from politics to mining. Despite his views, which often opposed Church interests and activities, an unusual respect developed between Connor and President Brigham Young.⁶¹ Late in his life, President Young said of Colonel Connor, "Men have been here before him; to our faces they were our friends; but when they went away they traduced, villified and abused us. Not so with Connor. We always knew where to find him. That's why I like him."⁶²

President Young died in August 1877, and Colonel Connor in 1891. Both men are buried in Salt Lake City: President Young in a private cemetery on his own farm site, now downtown Salt Lake City, and Patrick Connor at Fort Douglas, near the military site he initially established to keep an eye on the Saints.

Conclusion

War is miserable for those who survive it, support it, or endure it. It is much harder for those who actually participate in it—especially those who are its victims. From a gospel perspective, the Civil War was a brother-against-brother conflict in a spiritual and literal sense. The revelation received by the Prophet Joseph Smith that predicted "the death and misery of many souls" was literally fulfilled. Added to this measure of misery was the staggering economic cost to the nation as a whole.

Notwithstanding the costs of the Civil War, even its death and misery, "it is not right that any man should be in bondage one to another" (D&C 101:79), and the Civil War helped to determine that, at the very least, the institution of slavery would not continue as it existed prior to the conflict. For four million African-Americans, this meant freedom at last. As the nation bound up its wounds in the months and years that followed, the Church once again returned to the eastern United States and missionaries traveled the same paths that were the scenes of some of the greatest carnage in the nation's history. The gospel message again went forward in the valleys of death where the armies of the North and South battled to save the nation on God's promised land. The few Latter-day Saints who fought had a hand in preserving the United States of America for future generations. In the several decades following the war and leading up to statehood in Utah, the Saints' resolve to remain a part of that nation was sorely tested. In the end, however, Mormons went on to be blessed by the dividend of freedom which derived from the brutal conflict. Included in that dividend would be the protections offered up in the post–Civil War amendments that guaranteed rights to African-Americans and to those of other backgrounds, regardless of color or religion. It is a bold assertion but nonetheless true that the Church's ability to thrive was greatly assisted by the constitutional changes that came about in consequence of the war. Joseph Smith had once proclaimed himself "the greatest advocate of the Constitution of the United States there is on the earth." His only complaint was that it was "not broad enough to cover the whole ground."[63] Through the blessings secured by the civil rights amendments, particularly the Fourteenth Amendment, the nation he loved so dearly took major strides forward in securing the blessings of life, liberty, and the pursuit of happiness for all its citizens.

Notes

1. Henry Wells Jackson may have been the earliest Latter-day Saint soldier to die as a result of injury or disease (Saints at War Collection, Brigham Young University).

2. Brigham Young, quoted in Richard C. Bennett, *"We'll Find the Place": The Mormon Exodus, 1846–1848* (Salt Lake City: Deseret Book, 1997), 7.

3. Wilford Woodruff, January 1, 1871, in *Journal of Discourses* (London: Latter-day Saints' Book Depot, 1854–86), 14:2.

4. LaMar C. Berrett, "History of the Southern States Mission: 1831–1861" (master's thesis, Brigham Young University, 1960), 168–69.

5. In 1879, an aged local resident named Colonel Litz told two missionaries, Elders Mathias F. Cowley and Frank A. Benson, "that Elder Grant read to them in manuscript, the prophecy of Joseph Smith respecting the war of the rebellion, which took place over twenty years after Elder Grant read the revelation to the people of Tazewell County. They [the local people] derided the prophecy, but lived to see its verification written in letters of blood and tears" (in Berrett, "History of the Southern States Mission," 174).

6. Lycurgus A. Wilson, *Life of David W. Patten, The First Apostolic Martyr* (Salt Lake City: Deseret News, 1900), 62–63.

7. Wilford Woodruff, January 1, 1871, in *Journal of Discourses*, 14:3.

8. Joseph Smith, *History of the Church of Jesus Christ of Latter-day Saints*, ed. B. H. Roberts, 2nd ed. rev. (Salt Lake City: Deseret Book, 1957), 6:566.

9. Joseph Fielding Smith, *Church History and Modern Revelation* (Salt Lake City: Deseret News Press, 1947), 2:127–28.

10. The Civil War is known by several names, including the War Between the States, the War of Secession, the Great Revolt, and the War of Northern Aggression. These titles often reflect the interest or side represented by the individual referring to it. For the purpose of this paper, the Civil War or the Great War will be used.

11. The Prophet Joseph Smith's political position on slavery, which he articulated more than once, was clear: "Pray Congress to pay every man a reasonable price for his slaves out of the surplus revenue arising from the sale of public lands and from the deduction of pay from the members of Congress." Joseph also taught, "Break off the shackles from the poor black man, and hire him to labor like other human beings; for 'an hour of virtuous liberty on earth is worth a whole eternity of bondage'" (George Q. Cannon, *The Life of Joseph Smith the Prophet* [Salt Lake City: Deseret Book, 1964], 472–73).

12. *Church Almanac, 2006* (Salt Lake City: Deseret News, 2005), 250.

13. Robert Hall has identified approximately four hundred Latter-day Saints who participated in the war on one side or the other. Nearly one

hundred of this group were non-American convert immigrants who served in the war. This chapter touches on only a few, including John Evans, Henry Jackson, William Rex, and David H. Peery.

14. From 1841 to 1855, New Orleans was the principal port of arrival for Latter-day Saint converts who emigrated from Europe to the gathering places of the Saints in America. During this fourteen-year span, "17,463 immigrating saints arrived at the port of New Orleans" (Andrew Jenson, *Encyclopedic History of the Church of Jesus Christ of Latter-day Saints* [Salt Lake City: Deseret News, 1941], 576).

15. Mary A. Evans Thomas, "John Davis Evans," biographical sketch, Saints at War Collection, BYU, 1.

16. Thomas, "John Davis Evans," 1.

17. Thomas, "John Davis Evans," 1.

18. See Jerry Evan Crouch, *Silencing the Vicksburg Guns: The Story of the 7th Missouri Infantry Regiment As Experienced by John Davis Evans, Union Private and Mormon Pioneer* (Victoria, BC: Trafford, 2005), 13.

19. William Rex history, Saints at War Collection, BYU.

20. John C. Bennett to the editor of the *Times and Seasons*, signed "Joab, General in Israel," in *Times and Seasons*, November 1840, 205.

21. Abraham Lincoln to John T. Stuart, March 1, 1840, in Roy P. Basler, ed., *Collected Works of Abraham Lincoln* (New Brunswick: Rutgers University Press, 1953), 1:206; see also Cyril D. Pearson, "Abraham Lincoln and Joseph Smith," *Improvement Era*, February 1945, 103.

22. Heber J. Grant to Mr. Joy, February 12, 1941, Reel 126, Vol. 113, 622, Church Archives, The Church of Jesus Christ of Latter-day Saints, Salt Lake City.

23. Pearson, "Abraham Lincoln and Joseph Smith," 103.

24. Pearson, "Abraham Lincoln and Joseph Smith," 80.

25. May 1843, Smith, *History of the Church*, 5:394.

26. On June 12, 1857, after the prophecy was published, Senator Douglas, Democratic nominee for the United States presidency, delivered an address in Springfield, Illinois. After preferring several serious but

largely untrue charges against the Saints, Douglas stated, "Should such a state of things actually exist as we are led to infer . . . the knife must be applied to this pestiferous, disgusting cancer which is gnawing into the very vitals of the body politic. It must be cut out by the roots and seared over by the red hot iron of stern, unflinching law" (in Smith, *History of the Church*, 5:397).

27. Abraham Lincoln, quoted in Preston Nibley, *Brigham Young: The Man and His Works* (Salt Lake City: Deseret Book, 1965), 369.

28. Brigham Young, in *Journal of Discourses*, 9:5.

29. John Taylor, April 1861, in *Journal of Discourses*, 9:238.

30. John Taylor, in B. H. Roberts, *A Comprehensive History of The Church of Jesus Christ of Latter-day Saints* (Salt Lake City: Deseret News, 1930), 5:11.

31. Brigham Young, in *Journal of Discourses*, 10:273.

32. Southern converts and communities with an appreciable number of Southerners were scattered all over the Utah Territory. Colonies in the San Luis Valley of Colorado were settled specifically for the Southerners to help them avoid the persecution they experienced at home. Further, concentrations of Southern converts could be found in New Mexico, Arizona, Nevada, Utah, California, and Wyoming. Dr. Leonard J. Arrington has estimated that converts from the South never amounted to more than two percent of the Church's entire population, but the Southerners had a disproportionate impact upon the Church in the West in the areas of colonization, education, medicine, and missionary work. Although the estimate of two percent has been questioned, the impact of the Southerners on the Church has not (see David F. Boone, "Contributions of Southern Latter-day Saints for Their Church and the American West," unpublished manuscript presented at the Mormon History Association annual conference, Killington, Vermont, May 2005; see also Leonard J. Arrington, task paper, in author's possession).

33. While the political or religious persuasions of those involved cannot always be ascertained, Chad Orton is quick to suggest that some outbursts

were made as reckless affronts or "were made simply to annoy the troops" (Orton, "Away Down South in Dixie," unpublished manuscript prepared for the Mormon History Association meeting in Cedar City, Utah, May 2001, 19).

34. Orton, "Away Down South in Dixie," 10, 19–20.

35. A significant irony here is that in 1857–58 Albert Sidney Johnston, as the leader of federal troops in the Utah War, spoke vehemently about the treason he believed the Saints committed in defying the federal government "and that the man uttering them should himself . . . stand among the leaders of a gigantic rebellion against that [same] government, and become a leader of armies devoted to the destruction that Union." Further, General Johnston was "himself stricken in death at the head of an army on the very verge of victory over an army fighting for the life of the government, and the perpetuity of the Union" (in Roberts, *Comprehensive History of the Church*, 4:312).

36. Roberts, *Comprehensive History of the Church*, 4:543; italics removed.

37. Margaret M. Fisher, comp. and ed., *Utah and the Civil War: Being the Story of the Part Played by the People of Utah in That Great Conflict* (Salt Lake City: Deseret Book, 1929), 112.

38. Fisher, *Utah and the Civil War*, 112. This meant that the Burton Company was required to take all of their own supplies, including, in most cases, even the food for their animals.

39. Fisher, *Utah and the Civil War*, 112.

40. Fisher, *Utah and the Civil War*, 118.

41. Fisher, *Utah and the Civil War*, 119.

42. Fisher, *Utah and the Civil War*, 120–21.

43. Fisher, *Utah and the Civil War*, 123ff.

44. William Henry Hooper was Utah's second delegate to Congress and was apparently returning east to continue in congressional representation. Hooper was born in Dorchester County, Maryland, on December 25, 1813. He moved to Illinois, where he worked as a merchant and later as a steamboat captain on the Mississippi River. He immigrated to Utah in 1850 and

was elected as U.S. Senator. Hooper ultimately was elected as a delegate to Congress the 36th, 39th, 40th, 41st, and 42nd Congresses, where he strongly defended the territory's interests. Hooper died December 30, 1882, at sixty-nine years of age.

45. It should be remembered that Governor Alfred Cumming was appointed as the governor of Utah to replace Brigham Young, July 11, 1857. He was, however, with the troops in winter encampment until early April 1858, when he traveled to Salt Lake City and actually served as governor until Friday, May 17, 1861, when he and his wife left the territory quietly. Cumming was considered by the Saints to be a good leader who was stern but fair. He left because he felt an allegiance to his native Georgia and departed Utah only days after Fort Sumter was fired upon and the Civil War commenced. It was undoubtedly this departure that afforded President Young, rather than some government official, the opportunity to communicate with President Lincoln via the newly completed telegraph.

46. Fisher, *Utah and the Civil War*, 170.

47. Roberts, *Comprehensive History of the Church*, 4:550.

48. *Deseret News*, April 30, 1862, as quoted in Roberts, *Comprehensive History of the Church*, 4:550–51.

49. "Dispatch of L. Thomas, adjutant general, war department, Washington D.C., of 28th April, 1862," quoted in Roberts, *Comprehensive History of the Church*, 4:551; emphasis in original.

50. Fisher, *Utah and the Civil War*, 25.

51. Fisher, *Utah and the Civil War*, 25–26. While this promise was literally fulfilled, there were in fact deaths. In late July 1862, a part of the company on a mission stopped for a short rest, but there was little to eat since provisions were depleted. Seymour B. Young shared a small crust of dry bread with all of his associates, saying, "Here boys this is the best I can do for you." Private Donald McNicol remarked, "I do not mind starving, but I would hate to drown." Soon thereafter the company had to cross the south fork of the Snake River. Most of the men crossed safely but looked back to see McNicol disappear below the river's surface. "McNicol . . . was

seen to come to the surface and was swiftly carried with the current down the stream beyond all human aid." Ironically, McNicol was considered by his associates as "one [of] the best swimmers in the company" (Fisher, *Utah and the Civil War*, 78–79). Solomon Hale, who was in charge of the supply wagons and was tentmate with Lot Smith, remembered that the night after McNicol drowned, their commander "walked the camp all night, broken-hearted, because of the death of one of his men" (Fisher, *Utah and the Civil War*, 109). Mark Murphy, a teamster for the company, died due to exposure and hardships "endured while out in Government Service under Capt. Lot Smith." He died in December 1864, four months after the company's discharge (Fisher, *Utah and the Civil War*, 96). Private Moroni W. Alexander volunteered to save some of his company who were in grave danger of drowning, and "his body was torn and bruised from head to foot, lacerated from the force of the rocks striking against him" as he was carried by the wild river current. As a result of his heroic act, Alexander "contracted a severe cold . . . and a cough developed which remained with him all his life" (Fisher, *Utah and the Civil War*, 80).

52. Fisher, *Utah and the Civil War*, 99.
53. Fisher, *Utah and the Civil War*, 26.
54. Fisher, *Utah and the Civil War*, 39.
55. Fisher, *Utah and the Civil War*, 93.
56. Fisher, *Utah and the Civil War*, 96–97.
57. Fisher, *Utah and the Civil War*, 148–49, 111.
58. Fisher, *Utah and the Civil War*, 171.
59. Gustive O. Larson, *Outline History of Utah and the Mormons* (Salt Lake City: Deseret Book, 1958), 195.
60. Matthew P. Willden, "Connor Patrick E.," in *Encyclopedia of Latter-day Saint History*, ed. Arnold K. Garr, Donald Q. Cannon, and Richard O. Cowan (Salt Lake City: Deseret Book, 2000), 240.
61. While much of what President Young and Colonel Connor stood for and did for Utah seemed to be at odds with the other, a friendship developed between the two. In 1871 Church leaders, including Brigham

Young, "were arrested for 'lascivious co-habitation.'" Connor is said to have offered to furnish $100,000 bond for the Mormon leader" (E. B. Long, *The Saints and the Union: Utah Territory during the Civil War* [Urbana: University of Illinois Press, 1981], 270).

62. Long, *The Saints and the Union*, 270.

63. Joseph Smith, *Teachings of the Prophet Joseph Smith*, comp. Joseph Fielding Smith (Salt Lake City: Deseret Book, 1976), 326.

Introduction to the Spanish-American and Philippine Wars

"IT HAS BEEN A SPLENDID LITTLE WAR; BEGUN WITH THE HIGHEST MOTIVES, *carried on with magnificent intelligence and spirit, favored by that fortune which loves the brave."*
—*John Hay, American ambassador to Great Britain, to Colonel Theodore Roosevelt after the Spanish-American War*

SPAIN BEGAN ITS AMERICAN EMPIRE in 1492, when Christopher Columbus arrived in the West Indies. For nearly three centuries, Spain controlled vast areas in the Americas, but by the early nineteenth century Spain's power was waning and its colonies in the New World desired freedom. Inspired by the American Revolution and the French Revolution, people in Mexico and South and Central America revolted, and by 1825 freedom from Spain had been achieved. Spain's overseas empire was reduced to a few scattered islands. But it was not long until these islands also demanded their freedom from Spanish rule.

Cuba began its struggle for freedom in 1868, and rebels continued to fight until 1878, when a treaty was signed with the Spanish government. The treaty granted Cuba greater autonomy, but in reality very little changed. Cuban resistance revived in the 1890s under the leadership of José Martí, who had been living in exile in the United States. He returned to Cuba in 1895 to lead the resistance movement. This cry for independence caught the attention of the American people.

A Cry for Independence

During the second half of the nineteenth century, the United States was greatly influenced by the idea of manifest destiny. Once the American West had been subdued, many Americans looked to spread their influence to other parts of the world. Cuba drew a great amount of American interest because of the profitable sugarcane industry. This interest in Cuba prompted many Americans to call for U.S. intervention on behalf of the Cuban rebels, but in 1895 President Grover Cleveland declared neutrality. Tensions between the United States and Spain grew as the American public became aware of the Spanish policy of reconcentration, or the forced relocation of Cuban citizens. Spanish general Valeriano Weyler, in an attempt to quell the rebellion, began moving the Cuban population to the center of the island, placing them under guard and instituting martial law throughout the island. Relations between the U.S. and Spain continued to decline until February 15, 1898, when an explosion on board the USS *Maine* sank the ship in Havana Harbor. "Remember the *Maine*" soon became the rallying cry as popular support for war spread through the American public. On February 25, 1898, Congress declared war, and three days later the U.S. Navy created a naval blockade around Cuba. As the crisis continued to escalate in Cuba, tensions escalated in other parts of the world.

Resentment of Spanish rule had been growing in the Philippines, where guerrillas had been fighting against the Spanish throughout the 1890s. Though the events in Cuba started the war, the first fighting took place in the Philippines. Commodore George Dewey left Hong Kong two days after war was declared, and on May 1, 1898, he engaged a Spanish fleet at the Battle of Manila Bay. The U.S. forces annihilated the Spanish fleet, but Dewey did not have the troop strength to begin an invasion. Filipino guerrillas controlled land operations until U.S. forces arrived in July 1898.

> The attack was more costly than anticipated, and American casualties reached 1,385.

While Dewey was subduing the Spanish in the Philippines, the Spanish admiral Pascual Cervera sneaked through the U.S. blockade around Cuba. He entered the port at Santiago de Cuba but was quickly discovered and trapped in the port. The U.S. sent troops to Santiago de Cuba under the leadership of General William Shafter. Shafter arrived in June of 1898 and landed his forces near Daiquiri-Siboney, where they were joined by five thousand Cuban revolutionaries led by Calixto Garcia. Shafter began a westward march toward Santiago de Cuba. As U.S. forces approached Santiago de Cuba, they discovered that the Spanish were entrenched in a strong defensive position on the San Juan Heights. Shafter formed three divisions to attack the heights, which were the last obstacle preventing the capture of Santiago de Cuba. The attack began on July 1, 1898. Spanish artillery caused major problems for advancing American troops, but American Gatling guns were finally able to drive the Spanish from their positions and U.S. forces took the heights. The attack was more costly than anticipated, and American casualties reached 1,385 (with 205 dead). Shafter began a siege on the city of Santiago de Cuba, securing its surrender on July 17, 1898.

The loss in Cuba forced the Spanish government to enter peace negotiations, but while these negotiations were being held U.S. forces struck two more Spanish positions. General Nelson Miles led an expedition to Puerto Rico, where he encountered little opposition. U.S. forces also attacked Manila, but again they encountered little resistance. With the war essentially over, Spain agreed to end hostilities on August 12, 1898, and on December 10, 1898, Spain and the United States signed a peace treaty in Paris. The treaty granted independence to Cuba and ceded Puerto Rico and Guam to the United States. The U.S. also purchased the Philippine Islands from Spain for $20 million. Approximately three thousand American lives were lost in the war, though the vast majority were lost due to infectious diseases rather than to combat.

A Second War

American forces continued to fight in the Philippines for the next three years, as Filipino guerrillas fought for outright independence. The Filipinos fought bravely but did not have the necessary supplies to sustain the war effort. The conflict known as the Philippine War officially ended on July 4, 1902, though occasional skirmishes continued throughout the next decade. Another 1,037 American soldiers lost their lives in this conflict, bringing the total lives lost in the Spanish-American War and the Philippine War to roughly four thousand.

The United States worked to stabilize the government in the Philippines, eventually granting the Philippines independence in 1946, several decades after the war had ended. Guam and Puerto Rico, the other territories the United States gained in the war with Spain, remain U.S. territories to this day.

5

The Spanish-American and Philippine Wars

JAMES I. MANGUM

★ ★ ★

WHEN SENATOR JOSEPH RAWLINS stood on the Senate floor discussing Cuban affairs, he represented the feelings of many of his constituents in Utah. After the senator had laid out the nation's relationship with its Caribbean neighbor, he urged his colleagues to declare war on Spain without waiting for the actions of President William McKinley. Senator Rawlins's actions were prompted, at least in part, by the destruction of the USS *Maine*, a battleship docked in Havana Harbor.

James I. Mangum is an instructor for the Church Educational System.

Additionally, his argument pointed to the plight of Cubans who were facing incredible atrocities under the oppressive Spanish regime.[1] Although the resolution was not passed at that time, President McKinley addressed Congress six days later and received the authority to end the Spanish rule of Cuba with military force.[2]

With the United States at war, Utah was expected to take its place among military ranks. Since much of the state's population consisted of members of The Church of Jesus Christ of Latter-day Saints, Church leaders took a definite interest in supporting members involved in the hostilities. The fighting in this war affected the entire Church, even after the soldiers returned home. This influence was apparent in the attitudes of General Authorities toward the war, the success of the battalions that consisted mainly of Latter-day Saints, the attempts of continued missionary work, and the lives of future Church leaders who served during the war.[3]

The Church Takes a Stand

At the turn of the nineteenth century, Latter-day Saints were in a delicate position, one that divided the opinions of its members. Since the 1840s, they had struggled for statehood, only to have their petitions repeatedly rejected by the federal government.[4] Finally, in 1896, Utah received statehood, and only two years later the "baby state"—as the newest state was known at the time—was part of a nation on the brink of war. Like other Americans, individual Latter-day Saints held differing views of the impending conflict. Some felt it was time for the Latter-day Saints to help fight for the liberties of others. This opinion may have been influenced by the inflammatory newspapers of the day, but it did reflect the thoughts of many Latter-day Saints. Conversely, other Saints felt that their years of toil in the Rocky Mountains had earned them isolation from the violence of war. This seclusion had previously allowed them to avoid the destruction of lives that had occurred in the Civil War, and some felt that they could also avoid the present looming conflict. Saints on both sides of the issue eagerly awaited instructions from the Lord's prophet in the upcoming spring general conference.

The April conference of 1898 began ten days after the naval court of inquiry found that a submerged mine had destroyed the *Maine* as it was moored in Havana Harbor. During this time, Congress debated the nation's course of action in Cuba and with the Spanish government. The intense political situation inevitably permeated the addresses given in conference. President George Q. Cannon, First Counselor in the First Presidency, broached the subject by listing many of the current struggles in the world and their accompanying anxiety. He then explained that while Utah was part of the nation, Latter-day Saints did not share the fear exhibited by others throughout the country. His reason for the security felt by the Latter-day Saints was that they had God's prophet leading them. President Cannon then testified that "if there is any danger threatening us we shall be prepared for it. The Lord will inspire His servants and His people so that they will not be found unprepared."[5] His assurances were only the beginning of the discussion on the Church's stance on the war with Spain.

The fighting in this war affected the entire Church, even after the soldiers returned home.

The next morning, Elder Brigham Young Jr. provided another perspective on the subject of war. He exhorted the Latter-day Saints to worry more about spiritual preparation than about military preparation. He stated that one sign of the Savior's Second Coming was that every nation would be at war except for the people of Zion. Elder Young then wondered aloud about the traits of Zion that would allow it to remain at peace and then suggested that current practices among Church members did not reflect those traits. He counseled that "we have no time to spare; that the time is now when we must prepare ourselves, that when those who desire peace flee unto us they will not find us wanting."[6] Elder Young apparently felt that the Second Coming was imminent; therefore, he urged Saints to use all of their strength to prepare Zion instead of wasting that strength on war.

One strong reason for peace among the Latter-day Saints was the need for the continued work of missionaries. An international conflict would obviously hinder missionary work. Not only would potential missionaries have to risk their lives in battle, but missionaries already abroad would encounter increased hostility because of their nationality. B. H. Roberts, one of the Presidents of the Seventy, commented on how the Lord had opened the doors to missionary work throughout the world. He also suggested that the Latter-day Saints ought to retain their ability to do this work rather than involving themselves in the sin of war.[7] Elder Francis M. Lyman would later concur with Roberts's statements by adding, "We want peace, because we are a peaceable people, and we want to preach the Gospel. . . . That is our mission, and we don't want war."[8]

With the subjects of Zion and missionary work now on the minds of the members, President Wilford Woodruff arose on the third day of conference and gave a short speech that showed his insight into the fate of the Church and the world. President Woodruff related an experience he had not long after he had joined the Church. Parley P. Pratt had approached him and encouraged him to join the march of Zion's Camp. Just prior to leaving for Missouri, the Prophet Joseph Smith gathered the priesthood brethren together for a meeting. The Prophet instructed a few of the other brethren to share their testimonies of the work of the Lord. After listening to these witnesses, Joseph stood and said, "Brethren I have been very much edified and instructed in your testimonies here tonight. But I want to say to you before the Lord, that you know no more concern-

President Wilford Woodruff, circa 1890. © by Intellectual Reserve, Inc.

ing the destinies of this Church and kingdom than a babe upon its mother's lap. You don't comprehend it." President Woodruff related that he was rather taken aback at the time, but then the Prophet continued, "It is only a little handfull of Priesthood you see here tonight, but this Church will fill North and South America—it will fill the world." As President Woodruff looked at the body of Saints sitting before him in 1898, he knew that this prophecy of Joseph Smith had not yet been fulfilled. Still, he explained that it was currently being fulfilled because the Rocky Mountains were filling with Saints. However, he could not overlook that the Church had not yet "filled the whole earth" (Daniel 2:35). In his own way, Woodruff had taught that the Second Coming could not happen yet because there was so much missionary work still left to do.[9]

President Woodruff's subtle comments took a stand on the imminence of the Second Coming but left open the question of war. Throughout the rest of the conference, other speakers explained their understanding of how the members of the Church should view the world. Even in the last session, the Brethren had apparently not yet reached a consensus. Elder Franklin D. Richards said, "It seems as if the human family were anxious to become drunk with blood and imbrue their hands in each other's blood. And what a work will it be when peace is taken from the earth! Let us cultivate peace."[10] He was followed by President George Q. Cannon, who, as a member of the First Presidency, likely understood the views held by President Woodruff. He quoted Book of Mormon passages that promised the settlers of this land a continent without kings as long as the settlers remained righteous. He saw this war with Spain as an opportunity to rid the western hemisphere of an additional European monarch and thus fulfill God's word.[11] As two of the last three speakers in the conference session, Elder Richards and President Cannon still represented the opposite ends of the spectrum on this issue, perhaps mirroring the sentiments of Church members sitting in the pews.

These talks set the stage for President Woodruff to give his final address at general conference, in which he made an effort to reunite the Church on this issue. Modeling the principles taught in Doctrine and Covenants 121, President Woodruff shared another experience from his long life:

In April, 1838, while in the town of Kirtland, in walking across the street I met two men who held the Apostleship. They said to me, "Brother Woodruff, we have something that we want you to join us in." Said I, "What is it?" "We want another Prophet to lead us." "Whom do you want?" "We want Oliver Cowdery. Joseph Smith has apostatized." After listening to them, I said to them: "Unless you repent of your sins you will be damned and go to hell, and you will go through the fulness of eternal damnation, and all your hopes in this life will pass before you like the frost before the rising sun. You are false. Joseph Smith has not apostatized. He holds the keys of the kingdom of God on earth, and will hold them until the coming of the Son of Man, whether in this world or in the world to come." I am happy to say that those men did repent pretty soon, turned to the Church, and died in it.[12]

He then turned the subject to the Apostles sitting on the stand that day and remarked, "I do not believe the day will ever come—it is too late in the day, in my opinion—when any Elder in this Church will be called to stand before any two of the Apostles with us today and give unto them the declaration that I gave unto the two Apostles I have referred to. . . . I have faith to believe that these men who bear the Apostleship will hold it and live their religion. . . . I do not think that one of them will apostatize. I believe they will be with you and with this Church while they stand in the flesh, true and faithful to God."[13] These words give insight into the nature of Apostles and other General Authorities. Each individual had incredible leadership skills; such traits are necessary to lead the Lord's Church. President Woodruff knew the integrity of his colleagues and the strength of their characters, but he also needed them to support him even if he had different instructions. "By gentleness and meekness, and by love unfeigned" (D&C 121:41), President Woodruff reminded all Church leaders of their loyalty to the office which he held.

The prophet then took a stand on the subject of loyalty to the nation. He bore testimony of the righteousness of the Founding Fathers and described them as the best men that God could find on the earth. He stated that the Lord inspired these leaders, including George Washington, to establish this nation.[14] At that moment, President Woodruff, as future actions would also show, allied the Church with the United States of America. There was no more need to argue over where the Church would stand.

Still, the need for unity did not stop at the leadership of the Church, so President Woodruff turned his remarks to the general membership. "I feel," he announced, "as though the day has come when every Elder and every Latter-day Saint ought to stop and consider the position he is in and the covenants he has entered into. Is there anything on the face of the earth that will pay you to depart from the oracles of God and from the Gospel of Christ?"[15] President Woodruff, who had taught that "the Lord will never permit [him] or any other man who stands as President of the Church to lead you astray,"[16] once again urged them to follow the Lord's servants, even if they needed to change their opinions to do so. Indeed, President Cannon had been correct in stating that the Lord's prophet would lead them.

Showing Patriotism

Although President Woodruff had thrown the Church's lot in with the American government, his remarks did not explain just how the Church would show its loyalty. The need for clarity on that subject came only two days after the conference ended. On April 11, 1898, President McKinley went to Congress to ask for authorization to send troops to Cuba. His goal was to end Spanish rule there. On April 22, 1898, the U.S. Navy blockaded Cuba, and on April 25, Congress passed a bill that declared war on Spain. As citizens of the United States, the Latter-day Saints were at war.[17]

In the midst of these circumstances, Elder Brigham Young Jr. spoke in the Tabernacle on April 24. He taught that the Saints could show their patriotism in ways other than throwing away the lives of their sons. He suggested that the Saints raise money to pay for the war rather than send soldiers. In his speech, he said he was worried about the ravages of disease on Mormon men, whose constitutions were accustomed to the climate of the mountains of the West and not the swamps of Cuba.[18] He was certain that these illnesses would have more devastating consequences than the war itself.[19]

President Woodruff attended Elder Young's speech and the next day recorded the following response in his journal: "Mon[day] Ap[ril] 25 At the office [,] . . . I expressed my feelings in regard to Bro B. Youngs remarks at the Tabernacle yesterday as being unwise, as we are now a State & must take part either in peace or war and requested John Q Cannon to write a piece for publication in the *Deseret News* expressing my feelings, which he did."[20] President

No Disloyalty Here

"The Latter-day Saints, leaders and people, have ever believed that a time would come when it would be ther proud honor to defend and maintain the Constitution of the United States. They have been taught and universally believe that high Heaven inspired the fathers of the Republic. They have had the most exalted conceptions of the destiny of the Nation and of the profound and mighty part reserved to it among all the powers of the world. They are therefore absolutely loyal; their patriotism is not on a matter of practice and instinct—it is an essential feature of their religion, a part of their very life.

"Where they will stand in any emergency where patriotism is called for in maintaining the Nation's honor, can be no subject of doubt. This is their country—they are a portion of it, and in its defense none will be more ready to die if need be. Of the government they are a part, and as they love its institutions so will they sustain those institutions against every foe. An insult to that government is an insult to every true American, and in these mountain tops there is no lack of sturdy, God-fearing men ready to do their full and valiant duty in any such crisis whenever the call shall come. Not lovers of war, nor given to blood-thirstiness, they are nevertheless firmly and steadfastly with and for Our Country in every just cause— and he but poorly knows their heart and spirit who utters a word or harbors a thought that they are lacking in any element of the purest, staunchest and most enduring loyalty" (*Deseret Evening News*, April 25, 1898, 4).

Woodruff was able to see the big picture of the growth of the Church, and it required the help or at least the nonresistance of the U.S. government. Furthermore, he saw the speech given by Elder Young as a threat to the recently acquired peace between the Church and the United States. To solve the problem, Woodruff met with three members of the Young family: Elder Young; his brother, Major Willard Young; and their nephew, Captain Richard W. Young. The latter two were both members of the Utah National Guard. "The apostle was chastised for speaking without authorization and was told not to oppose the enlistment of Mormon volunteers."[21] To his credit, Elder Young fell in line with the instructions of his leader. Months later he would take particular interest in the soldiers and, through the help of Captain Young, institute a program to maintain the soldiers' spiritual strength.[22]

Captain Richard W. Young, circa 1900. Courtesy of University of Utah.

That same day, the First Presidency sent out several other letters that explained the Church's stance on members enlisting in the armed services. First, a letter was sent to Governor Heber M. Wells. In that letter, the presidency explained that the Church was against war and that its responsibility was to proclaim peace. Yet in the current circumstances they also felt it their duty to support the war effort.[23] Next, President George Q. Cannon wrote a letter to all of the stake presidents of the Church. President Cannon instructed these leaders not to impede the work of recruitment among their members. Conversely, they were to encourage the enlistment of

Utah Battery A takes artillery practice outside Salt Lake City. Courtesy of Church Archives.

Latter-day Saint soldiers for the conflict. By sending their message out on several fronts, Church members no longer had to guess at the Church's position on the war.

Involvement of the Church in the Spanish-American War followed a precedent set by previous latter-day prophets. While individual Saints were allowed their own opinions, the needs of the Church were studied and the course of action that would best serve the mission of the Church was chosen. Then the President of the Church would come forward and lead the Saints in the way the Lord would have them go. In the case of the Spanish-American War, President Woodruff encouraged the Saints to be loyal to their nation.

The Saints Join the Fight

With the nation at war, over five hundred Latter-day Saints stepped forward to fight for a cause they thought was just. For example, Stephen Bjarnson, a youth from Spanish Fork, explained to a friend that he did not join the army because he was thirsty to shed blood. Instead, he explained that the Spanish had shed innocent blood for centuries and that this continued with their oppression of the Cubans. So he felt it was his duty as a free person to step forward and protect the liberty of others.[24]

Willard Call, from Bountiful, Utah, also stepped forward to offer his services, then went to his wife to learn her opinion on his decision. She felt that she could support him in his decision if they had the Church's blessing. With that in mind, they went to visit President George Q. Cannon and ended up meeting with the entire First Presidency. President Wilford Woodruff gave his support, saying, "If you go, you will go with our blessings and the blessings of the Lord will attend you." With this encouragement Willard joined the United States Volunteers that very day.[25]

The initial request from the military was that Utah enlist and organize men into two artillery batteries and one troop of cavalry. These three organizations would be made up of five hundred men. However, so many men wanted to fight for their country that another troop of cavalry was organized. The governor received special permission to maintain the second cavalry force. In addition, Utah provided a third artillery battery, a troop of supply packers, and various other soldiers to the regular army. The three Utah units were mostly made up of Latter-day Saint soldiers. The national newspaper *Harper's Weekly* reported, "About two-thirds of the men in the [Utah] batteries are Mormons—members of leading families in the Church."[26] Once the Church had put forward its stance on the war, members of the Church joined the army in great numbers.[27]

Utah Volunteer regiments march in a parade through San Francisco before leaving for the Philippines. Courtesy of Church Archives.

Reluctant Chaplain

The outbreak of the Spanish-American War found Elias S. Kimball (younger brother of Elder J. Golden Kimball of the Seventy) in Tennessee. He was serving as the president of the Southern States Mission and was enjoying great success. He had instituted a program in which his missionaries would travel without purse or scrip, forcing them to rely on the mercy of the Lord in their work. It was later remarked that "Elder Elias Kimball . . . was a very pronounced believer in the idea that a missionary's usefulness did not commence until he had been deprived of every human prop and support, and had been compelled to place his trust solely in the strength of God."²⁸ The Lord would test Kimball's trust with a call to become the first Latter-day Saint chaplain.

Ironically, the day the call to the chaplaincy arrived, Elias Kimball and his older brother J. Golden had spent the morning in Chattanooga watching the soldiers parade in the streets. On returning to the mission office, Elias found the letter from Church headquarters. This letter began by releasing Elias from his position as mission president and then extending another call: "The Presidency had been invited by [Colonel] Willard Young of the 2nd Regiment Volunteer Engineers to name the Chaplain for his regiment, and the question was considered at to-day's meeting. It was unanimously decided to recommend you for that position, and Col. Young was informed of this by telegram to-day. He is at present at Washington, D.C., and you are requested to report by letter to him, care of Senator [Frank] J. Cannon, if you feel to accept of the appointment."²⁹ While the new assignment was a shock to Kimball, he was more surprised by his release as mission president. He knew that the release was coming, but he had not expected it to happen until the autumn of that year.

Elias S. Kimball, former president of the Southern States Mission and first Latter-day Saint chaplain, 1897. Courtesy of Church Archives.

J. Golden Kimball, in an attempt to comfort his younger brother, explained that Elias was lucky to have received another calling at the time of his release because his testimony would not stagnate because of disuse. Elias tried to take this encouragement to heart, but he found it difficult to leave the work in which he was engaged.[30]

That evening Elias had his first experience with military ignorance of Latter-day Saint customs. Elias and J. Golden returned into town to eat supper and discuss the new call as chaplain. While at the restaurant they started a conversation with a couple of army officers. Elias inquired about the position of chaplain and explained that he was going to become one. While explaining the position, they repeatedly mentioned that the position was for ordained clergy. That evening Elias had been wearing a light-colored coat, not the black coat with white collar that the officers expected. From the beginning, Elias Kimball knew he would have to teach others about priesthood authority and the absence of a paid clergy in the Church.

The next day, Elias sat at his typewriter and composed a couple of letters, signifying his obedience to the call. First he sent a letter to Church headquarters to say that he accepted his new assignment. Next he wrote to Colonel Young and shared the same message. Although Elias was not excited about the change, he was now committed to serve as the first Latter-day Saint chaplain in the U.S. Army as long as the commission had been made by President William McKinley.

In the time between the call from the First Presidency and the letter of appointment from the president of the United States, Elias took his family home to Mendon, Utah. The official appointment letter was slow in coming, and Elias ended up getting a sales position—selling Studebakers—while he waited. However, a short time later, a reporter from the *Salt Lake Tribune* arrived at his home. The reporter had received a cable that President McKinley had appointed

Colonel Willard Young, 2nd Regiment Volunteer Engineers, 1898. Courtesy of Church Archives.

Elias to serve as a chaplain, and now the reporter wanted to interview the new appointee. Elias gave him a life sketch, and the man drew Elias's likeness, which appeared in the *Tribune* on June 19, 1898.[31] When a telegram from Colonel Young confirmed the appointment, Kimball remarked, "This information dispelled all doubt as to my going. Shall go Saturday or Sunday." In addition, Elias's journals show that he had hoped that the president would not make this appointment. He would rather have stayed in Utah and sold Studebakers. However, since he had been called by a prophet and appointed by a president, Elias prepared to go to war.

To get to Illinois, Kimball had to board a train in Salt Lake City. The nervous recruit wanted to be set apart in his new calling, so he went to Church headquarters. Under the direction of President Joseph F. Smith, Elder Franklin D. Richards set Elias apart. That night he recorded portions of his blessing in his journal: "Bro. Richards was mouth and gave me a most excelent [*sic*] blessing. . . . Brother Richards . . . said that I should prove a great blessing to the 2nd Regiment and those [that Kimball] blessed should be blessed and that Col. Young and the officers and men would feel blessed by my presence among them."[32] Kimball shared that he was glad because much of the blessing echoed a blessing written by his older brother.[33] With these blessings in his mind, Elias began his military experience.

After arriving in Illinois, Kimball was introduced to Colonel Young's staff, and within a few days he was in uniform. The colonel pulled Kimball aside before the latter's first sermon and explained how to give a sermon to soldiers. The message had to be nondenominational, and it had to be short; otherwise the chaplain might lose his audience. The colonel then gave Kimball twenty minutes to share his message. The chaplain responded, "I did not intend to preach anything not contained in the scriptures, but . . . follow the direction of the holy Spirit."[34] Kimball was so nervous of overstepping his bounds that he took less than twenty minutes. This was not the last time that military dictates prescribed how the chaplain performed his duties. As Young's unit of engineers moved to Florida and later to Cuba, more Sundays than not would pass without a message being shared.

A few months later, Kimball voiced his frustration about the obstacles that prevented him from doing his job. He shared that irritation by quoting from a news article written by Reverend Sam Small, another chaplain. The article explained that chaplains were members of military units by name only. They had no authority and could not do much to decide when a religious meeting should be held. Even when meetings did occur, attendance was sparse. Kimball explained that he wholeheartedly agreed with Small's sentiments.

Kimball completed the rest of his service in this manner, but the reluctant chaplain was more than ready to return home when the time came. In his short service, Elias S. Kimball helped to open a new door for the Church: Latter-day Saint chaplains were now a part of the military, and they did not necessarily need to be attached to a unit from Utah. Future military conflicts would see a growth in the number of Latter-day Saint chaplains.

The Famous Battery Boys

In the decades before the turn of the twentieth century, the distinctive practices of the Latter-day Saints, including plural marriage, often fell under intense national scrutiny. When criticized for their beliefs, Church members defended their position and, like all people who truly cherish their ideas, held on to them even more fiercely. This, however, only earned the Saints a reputation of peculiarity and isolationism. This reputation stayed with the Church even after Utah was accepted into the Union. Yet, when the United States declared war on Spain, members of the Church had an opportunity to change the nation's attitude toward them by participating in the military. The actions of these men influenced the way others viewed Utah and the Church.

Most Latter-day Saint soldiers who saw battle did not face their foes in Cuba. Instead, they traveled thousands of miles to represent their country in the Philippines. One may wonder how the battle for the liberation of Cuba included the Pacific islands. Shortly after the declaration of hostilities between the two countries, U.S. commodore George Dewey received instructions to sail to the Philippine Islands. His orders included the following directions: "Commence operations particularly against the Spanish fleet. You must capture vessels or destroy. Use utmost endeavour."[35] Dewey's small fleet of

LDS Press Release:
Utahns in Spanish-American War
Invent "Artillery Charge"

"The scene is the jungle depths of the Philippine island of Luzon; the time is February 6, 1899; a war is under way—Americans against the Filipino insurgents. Commanding the American forces is General [Arthur] MacArthur, father of the present general. An artillery duel is being waged, and, in another strange parallel to present events, American guns are hitting their mark with uncanny accuracy, pounding enemy breastworks, silencing enemy batteries.

"Feeding shells to the battery of light artillery are the veterans of Battery A of the Utah Volunteers, commanded by Major Richard W. Young of Salt Lake City. According to the files of the Utah Writers' Project, gun crews were directed by Lieutenants George W. Gibbs and W. C. Webb, both of Salt Lake City.

"By 1:30 p.m. insurgent fire has almost ceased. American infantry receive orders for an advance on enemy positions. Lieutenant Webb swung to his men. 'Come on,' he said, 'let's go.' [']Hay! Lieutenant Gibbs! Let's go with the charge.'

'And leave the guns?' Gibbs called back.

'Hell no, we'll take 'em with us! Come on men! Get on the wheels. Let's roll down this hill!'

"An[d] then was enacted one of the most remarkable scenes ever witnessed on a battlefield; it was the first artillery charge in history, and likely the last, but it won the day! The Utah batteries wheeled their cannon along with the front line "stopping," as Lieutenant Webb recorded, "now and then to fire on the natives to start them running." Horrified natives broke cover under the spray of close range artillery shrapnel, and the American infantry picked them off with rifle fire. The enemy breastworks were taken without the loss of a man from the batteries.

"According to all military rules and traditions, the place for the artillery was in the rear. It had probably never occurred to any military man to lead a charge with a battery of light cannon. But Lieutenant Webb and the Utah boys thought it was the most natural thing in the world. Webb said later, 'We just went along with the firing line.' Just like that, no heroics, no color; he merely thought it was part of the day's work. This is the sort of thing which has been lauded as the heroic 'initiative' of the American Soldier" (Utah Writers' Project, Press Release, January 23, 1942).

Utah Light Artillery, by Keith Rocco. Courtesy of Utah National Guard.

ships had astounding success in Manila Harbor, as they succeeded in destroying all of the Spanish ships stationed there. Yet, having taken the harbor, Dewey did not have the manpower to capture the city. After receiving Dewey's request for more soldiers, the United States military prepared to send men to the Philippines, including Utah's A and B Light Infantry Batteries.[36]

The caliber of these units, primarily composed of Latter-day Saints, was exhibited by their leaders—Captain Richard W. Young and Captain Frank A. Grant. While Captain Grant was not a member of the Church, he was highly praised by those who served under him. He did not act like many other officers but seemed to understand the needs of his men.[37] Young also commanded respect. Wesley E. King, who served under Young's command, fit the common stereotype of a soldier as being crisp and cold. He then explained that

Young was not this way but that his men could see his warm heart in all that he did. While the captain could perform all the stiff actions of an officer, he led in a way that exhibited gentleness and kindness. King remembered one time when Young reprimanded him. He said, "That rebuke was filled with such kindness, such a tenderness of feeling toward me that I could not but bless him for it, and I did. His rebuke showed me at once the impossibility of such a thing being repeated and at the same time the pain to him in having to mention it."[38] With such leadership, it is not surprising that Utah's batteries were so successful.

After arriving in the Philippines, these soldiers took part in not only removing the Spanish army but also in putting down the Filipino insurrection. The conditions on the battlefield were dangerous, and the Utahns were able to distinguish themselves while performing their duties. On August 7, 1899, the *Salt Lake Herald* listed several of the heroic deeds performed by Utah Latter-day Saints. For example, Battery B sergeant Andrew Petersen was fatigued from crossing two miles of jungle and swamp while fighting, yet he was still able to put his cannon to good use. Another artillery soldier, Corporal J. W. Meranda shot his cannon so well that it sent a large group of Filipinos running. Adding to the difficulty of this battle, it was reported that so many bullets were flying during that

A General to His Men

Wars, by their very nature, cost a great deal of lives, both small and great. At the funeral of General Richard W. Young, Elder Melvin J. Ballard explained why some of the great Latter-day Saint soldiers are taken from this earth:

"He [Young] has been called to a greater field of usefulness and activity than that in which he could have engaged here, and it was burned into my soul that he died a great general and that assembled under the care of our Father and those with whom he is associated in the other world, were countless thousands, yea, hundreds of thousands of those brave soldiers who fell in this last great struggle. God wanted a great general among them; not only a lawyer and a soldier but a man like him, bearing the power and the authority of the holy priesthood, to preside over and minister among them, where he would be honored, where he would be recognized" (*Brigadier General Richard W. Young In Memoriam: Biographical Sketch, Funeral Ceremonies, Resolutions of Respect* [Salt Lake City: n.p., 1920], 15).

particular battle that one "might have swung a cup around and got it filled with lead." It was the bravery and skill shown in these times of great distress that caused the military to promote many of the Saints in the Utah batteries.[39]

Such deeds may have stood out by themselves, but these were not the only battles in which Latter-day Saints fought. When the war broke out, the government had reviewed their artillery units and found them to be severely lacking. Most units had only a handful of outdated cannons left over from the Civil War. Utah, however, was in a different position. When the state first entered the Union, the leaders of the National Guard were able to make use of surplus government funds and purchase their own guns.[40] So when the war started in Cuba, Utah's state-of-the-art artillery batteries were needed in the field. When they finally arrived in the Philippines, they spent every evening in the trenches because they were the only artillery units on the island.[41] Without the artillery support of the Utah units, the battle for Manila and the surrounding areas could not have been won.

In addition to the bravery shown in the destruction of enemy combatants, Latter-day Saint soldiers also performed actions that saved the lives of many of their fellow Americans. A soldier from Oregon remembered the heroism of one of these soldiers, Harvey Dusenberry:

> Dusenberry saved 100 Oregon soldiers from death and mutilation. The Oregonians . . . had been caught in an ambuscade where they were exposed to murderous fire from three sides. They could not extricate themselves, nor could they see their enemy. All that was permitted them was to stand up like American soldiers and blindly fight a concealed foe so long as life remained to them.
>
> Dusenberry, then a corporal of Battery B, saw the terrible position of the Oregonians from an elevation. He secured help

An artillery shell explodes near one of the Utah Battery's positions. Courtesy of Church Archives.

and drew up a Hotchkiss gun on the hill, whence he was able to pour a fire into the treacherous Filipinos. He kept up the cannonade for two hours, all the time exposed to a galling return fire. Fortunately he escaped unhurt, and was able to extricate the Oregon men from their dangerous position.

The newspaper reporter then conceded that there were probably scores of similar actions unreported, but these soldiers "with that modesty which is characteristic of the hero . . . have refrained from telling their stories of adventure." The story of Corporal Dusenberry may have met the same fate had it not been for the report made by the grateful Oregonian he had rescued.

For all of the fame won by members of the Church on the battlefield, the desire for fame was not the reason these young men had come to the Philippines. They had a duty to perform and they knew that others needed them to succeed. Frank T. Gines explained this duty in a song he wrote called "Battle Song of Utah."

> Clear the guns for action boys, we are brave and strong and true,
> Rouse and do the noble deeds you came so far to do.
> Strike a blow of vengeance for our murdered boys in blue,
> While we are fighting at Manila.
>
> *Chorus*
> Hurrah! Hurrah! for Utah and her crew,
> Hurrah! hurrah! for Pennsylvania too.
> We'll give them what we said we would, when first we donned the blue
> While we are fighting at Manila.[42]

Yet despite their desire to simply do their duty, others noticed their gallantry. Shortly before the two batteries returned to Utah, the *Deseret Evening News* interviewed Captain Frank Jennings, who had recently returned from duty in the Philippines. When asked about Utah's volunteers, he became quite enthusiastic and praised the work they had done. He explained that these soldiers had won a great deal of respect from their fellow soldiers in the Pacific. "In all the time he was on the island, he never heard the mention of our batteries, but what a response came breathing out the highest praise and love. Civilians and soldiers, officers and privates, regulars and volunteers, vie with each other in lauding Utah's valorous sons; they look upon them as a band of dauntless heroes, whose only watchword is duty, and in whom the element of fear has been expunged." Jennings then explained that the state of Utah could not honor these men too much because they had given the state a remarkable reputation.[43]

Other praise came from those a little closer to home. Reed Smoot, U.S. senator and member of the Quorum of the Twelve, gave a glowing review of the soldiers on the Senate floor in Washington DC. The hardest-won compliments came from the editor of the *Salt Lake Tribune*, Judge C. C. Goodwin. Even with his anti-Mormon bias, Goodwin had nothing but admiration for the Utah batteries, despite the number of Latter-day Saints in their ranks.[44] In addition to local praise, the heroic acts of these batteries were found in the pages of the *National Tribune*, *Harper's Weekly*, and other national newspapers.[45] Of particular note, the *New York World* made this statement about the state of Utah: "Our latest state has borne its share in adding to the glory of the nation. In the battle of Malate the Utah light artillery, whose guns were dragged through deep mud to send shrapnel into the Spaniards' ranks, showed itself deserving of all honor. Utah has had its troubles in the past, but when she sends such a contribution to the nation we wipe out the memory of all troubles."[46] Even the national press recognized that Utah, and therefore the Latter-day Saints, could make a major contribution to the welfare of the nation.

The reputation earned by Latter-day Saint artillery batteries began to change the way that the nation viewed the Church. The soldiers in the Philippines had an opportunity to learn about the Latter-day Saints, which, as Captain Jennings reported above, was a favorable experience. It also served to put the nickname of the Church, the Mormons, in print, and usually in positive circumstances. This positive press exposure helped change many Americans' attitudes toward the Church.

Praise to the Valor of LDS Soldiers

"The necessities of the war made them ubiquitous; they were everywhere, on river, on land; and when a stronghold was to be stormed, their guns first cleared the way, until, in an army where all were heroes, the men of Utah made for themselves a conspicuous name. They earned it, for they never retreated, never lost a battle or a flag, never started for the foe that they did not scatter it as the wind scatters the chaff from the threshing floor. When their terms of enlistment expired they fought on, week after week, until their places could be supplied. The record of the volunteers is nowhere dimmed. They went away boys; they returned men. They made for themselves great names, and by their deeds exalted the name of their state. They have won for themselves an appreciative people's gratitude, a nation's praise" (Judge C. C. Goodwin, *Salt Lake Tribune* editor, as quoted in B. H. Roberts, *Comprehensive History of the Church of Jesus Christ of Latter-day Saints* [Salt Lake City: Deseret News, 1957], 6:458).

The Mutual Improvement Association of the Far East

Leaving the boundaries of Utah did not mean leaving the Church behind. While serving their country, these men did not forget their religion but looked for ways to maintain their beliefs while abroad. They even attempted to operate key programs like those at home in order to ease their separation from friends and loved ones.

Shortly after they finished their training in their home state, the Utah batteries went to California in preparation to depart to the Philippines. While camped in the Presidio, they were visited by Ephraim H. Nye, president of the California Mission. While visiting with the Latter-day Saint soldiers, he encouraged them to start up a group to help them live their religion. Obviously President Nye was not the only one who desired to see an organization put together for the spiritual growth of the Latter-day Saint soldiers. Before the units even reached Hawaii, Major Young called George A. Seaman into his quarters on the transport ship. The officer had a letter in his hand from Brigham Young Jr. instructing him to have some sort of organization put together for religious purposes. Major Young called Seaman to organize that group. While Seaman felt overwhelmed, he told Young that he would do it. Before they reached the Philippines, thirty-seven men had agreed to the idea.

After the Battle of Manila and before the Filipino insurrection, the Latter-day Saint soldiers lived in the barracks, an arrangement that allowed George Seaman to finally organize a group to facilitate the soldiers' spiritual growth. On September 21, 1898, Seaman and a few others met and created what was referred to as the "Young Men's Mutual Improvement Association of the 'Far East.'"[47] This group met almost every week until the Filipino insurrection broke out in the early months of 1899.

While in the islands, the members of the MIA attempted to follow many of the programs used by the MIA in the United States. The main focus was on the study of the scriptures, particularly the

Acts of the Apostles. The MIA committee assigned passages to be read and then discussed them the following week, either as a group or as a lesson taught by one of the association members. In addition, they found several men to give speeches on various topics, ranging from the history of the Philippines and Spain to aspects of Christianity and Islam. In keeping with the practices of their associations at home, membership was open to members and non-members alike. Many commended this open-door policy and joined the organization.

The Mutual Improvement Association eased the lives of the men in Manila.

The MIA had another class that served as a motivation to join the association. Corporal George S. Backman, a student of the Spanish language, offered to teach a class on that subject. The only stipulation for attendance was that students be members of the MIA. This class was also successful enough that it lasted the several months prior to the insurrection.[48]

The MIA eased the lives of the men in Manila. Private Charles R. Mabey related that "after the singularities of his new surroundings had ceased to be uncommon he began to look about himself in search of other amusement."[49] For a bored soldier, the Philippines offered many ways to get in trouble, from cockfights to local women to alcohol. These behaviors worried general Church leaders and motivated them to have a spiritual group organized. While the meetings occurred only once a week, they had a long-lasting effect on some of the men in the batteries. In his journal, Mabey confided that his experiences in the association—both in listening and preparing presentations—helped increase his understanding of the scriptures. He also spoke of the personal growth he felt from attending the MIA.

The Church did not send out these men without ecclesiastical direction. Interviews with Willard Call and George A. Seaman relate that both of these men were set apart as missionaries to the Philippines on May 5, 1898. Seaman was set apart by Elder Owen Woodruff.[50] This explains why Young would single out Seaman to set up a Church organization among his men. Willard Call was set apart by Elder John Henry Smith of the Quorum of the Twelve Apostles. In his diary, Call declared, "I claim the distinction of being the first Mormon Elder to preach the Gospel among those Roman Catholic people in the Philippine Islands. I preached in Cortel de Mesic about August 30th 1898."[51] Through the work of these two men, both with the MIA and missionary work, the restored gospel was first taught in the Philippines.[52]

The Philippine Supreme Court

Near the end of 1898, newly promoted Major Richard Young received a new assignment from the U.S. government. A new government was needed once the Philippines had been defeated, and the army was not prepared to provide one. Instead, General Elwell S. Otis searched the ranks of the military for men who could fill the needed positions. He chose Young, a Columbia-trained lawyer, to help with many of the legal matters. Young had even spent a period of time before the insurrection as the judge of the Superior Provost Court.[53]

After the end of the war, the government of the United States asked for Young's service again. This time it appointed him to the supreme court of the Philippine Islands. His particular position on the bench was president of the Criminal Division, where he authored General Order 58. This order gave defendants in Filipino courts the "basic rights and procedures of an Anglo-Saxon Criminal Law." This replaced the inquisitorial practices of the Spanish government with a system that respected the rights of the accused. Within a few years, every lawyer in the islands was familiar with this document, and many applied it in behalf of their clients.[54] In a unique manner, Major Young was able to help obtain freedoms for the people of the Philippines.

Justice Young's work in the Philippines produced another unexpected benefit for the Church. General Otis was replaced as governor-general by a man with aspirations to the U.S. Supreme Court, William Howard Taft. Despite differences in political affiliations, Young was able to win the respect and trust of Governor Taft. President Heber J. Grant later remarked that "William H. Taft . . . ever afterwards was a friend not only of Richard W. Young, but of the Mormon people."[55] Such close ties helped the Church years later when Taft was elected president of the United States.

Compassionate Women

Much has been said about the accomplishments of Latter-day Saint men during this conflict, but it is also important to look at the work of compassionate women during this time. The men would not have lasted long without the encouragement of their loved ones. As mentioned, it was the support of his wife that allowed Willard Call to enlist and then serve as a soldier and a missionary in the Philippines. This support continued in the Philippines as the men received letters from home. Charles R. Mabey recalled the "magic of that one word 'Mail!'"[56] These acts of service bolstered the men and allowed them to do their duty.

However, this was only the beginning of the service provided by Latter-day Saint women during the war. From the time the men began to assemble at Fort Douglas in Salt Lake City, the women of that city found ways to make the soldiers' lives bearable. They provided fruits and vegetables to the men and then raised money, which they sent to the soldiers' families to ease any hardships. This led to the organization of the Salt Lake chapter of the Red Cross. These hardworking women continued to look after the physical needs of the men. They made over "376 bandages and 71 comfort bags, containing buttons, white and black thread, pins, safety pins, needles, fine comb, knife, fork, spoon, etc."[57]

The women of other cities were not to be outdone, and other chapters of the Red Cross were organized. From around Utah, Latter-day Saint women continued to donate money and goods. Then when the circumstances allowed it, they put on lunches for the men to give

> The women of other cities were not to be outdone. From around Utah, Latter-day Saint women continued to donate money and goods.

them a break from army food. Their work did not cease once the men had left the boundaries of the state but continued throughout the war. Additionally, when the men returned from the Philippines, they were treated to two separate receptions. After the men arrived in Ogden, the Red Cross put on a grand breakfast in Lester Park.[58] For two hours, the men ate and rejoiced at being home.[59] Then another homecoming party was organized at Liberty Park in Salt Lake City. The women of the Red Cross had supported their men in uniform from their first moments until their final return. They played a major part in helping the men to perform their duties.

Leadership from the Spanish-American War

The Spanish-American War did not affect the Church only during the years of actual conflict. It continued to touch the lives of Latter-day Saints after the soldiers returned home and took up positions of leadership both in the Church and in the community. The lives and points of view of these men changed during their time in the service, and they would use that perspective in future decisions. In addition to high-ranking military officers, ecclesiastical leaders and a future state governor would derive from the ranks of Latter-day Saint soldiers.

Stake presidents. Two Spanish-American War officers were later called to serve as stake presidents. After his service as the Church's first chaplain, Elias S. Kimball was called to serve as the first president of the Blackfoot Idaho Stake in January 1904.[60] A few months later, on April 1, Richard W. Young was set apart as the first president of the Ensign Stake in Salt Lake City.[61] At his funeral, his counselor John M. Knight described the leadership style of President Young: "He has been a friend to the friendless; he has been all that he could be to those who were in distress. I have seen him put his arms around a little waif in the street, whose feet were bare in the winter time, and take him to the great store, Z.C.M.I., and buy him shoes and clothing in order that he might be warm. I have gone with him to the home of a widowed mother, whose children had become wards of the juvenile court, and he put his arms around them and was endeavoring to make them live the lives of Latter-day Saints."[62] After the time these men spent in the service of their countries, the Lord saw fit to trust them with more of His kingdom.

Utah's fifth governor. Along with their ecclesiastical service, Latter-day Saint veterans of the Spanish-American War worked as public officials. Two decades after returning home from the Philippines—and after service as a major in World War I—Charles R. Mabey ran for the Utah governor's office. He had previously spent time as the mayor of Bountiful, Utah, and then later in the state legislature. The economic climate of the state and the nation helped to make Mabey the fifth governor of Utah. Latter-day Saint statesman Charles R. Mabey continued to make an impact in the lives of Church members after he returned home from the war.

Almost an Apostle

"Heber J. Grant was ordained and set apart as the seventh President of the Church on November 23, 1918. As he and his counselors, Anthon H. Lund and Charles W. Penrose, considered filling the vacancy in the Twelve caused by President Grant's ordination, they focused on Richard W. Young, grandson of Brigham Young and Heber's lifelong friend. A retired general of the army, a lawyer, and a former stake president, he had every qualification to serve in the Twelve. Deciding he was the man, President Grant wrote Richard W. Young's name on a slip of paper before going to the temple meeting where filling the vacancy was to be discussed. In the temple, he removed the paper with the name written on it, fully intending to present Richard W. Young to the council for approval. But for a reason he could never fully explain, he was unable to do so; instead, he presented the name of Melvin J. Ballard, president of the Northwestern States Mission, a man with whom he had had very little personal contact. This experience had a profound influence on President Grant. It taught him to heed the sudden flashes of insight that came to him in making decisions affecting the Church" (Francis M. Gibbons, *Dynamic Disciples, Prophets of God: Life Stories of the Presidents of the Church of Jesus Christ of Latter-day Saints* [Salt Lake City: Deseret Book, 1996], 169–70).

Conclusion

When war broke out in Cuba in 1898, the Church was in the capable hands of inspired leaders. While these leaders held their own opinions, President Wilford Woodruff prophetically explained the path that Latter-day Saints would need to take during the United States' involvement in this war. While he understood that many of the Saints were anxious for the coming of Christ, he also understood that the time was not yet near. His understanding is illustrated by his experience with several nervous members of the Church who had asked him when the Savior would return. President Woodruff reportedly answered, "I would live as if it were to be tomorrow—but I am still planting cherry trees!"[63] While the time would come that the Latter-day Saints and every other lover of peace would need to flee to Zion, that time had not yet arrived. Church policy, when it came to the Spanish-American War, would reflect the need for patriotism and the support of one's own country.

The Church's stance on the war was reflected in the instructions given to Church leaders, both at the general and local levels. General Authorities

A special homecoming parade was held for the returning Utah Volunteers in downtown Salt Lake City. Courtesy of Church Archives.

were instructed on the Church's position and were expected to support it. Local leaders were to encourage Saints to enlist. The Church even called the first Latter-day Saint chaplain, Elias S. Kimball, which spread the spiritual influence of the Church to the U.S. military. Kimball would serve as an example to subsequent chaplains, who would seek to bring the gospel of peace into the terrors of war.

The number of Utahns who enlisted in the armed forces exceeded the requirements made by the United States government.[64] Members of the Church demonstrated their willingness to serve their country by enlisting in military service. Later, when Utah's artillery battalions fought in the Philippines, they performed in such a way as to improve the reputation of the Latter-day Saints nationwide.

Off the battlefield, soldier-missionaries continued to spread the gospel through preaching and by the introduction of the Young Men's Mutual Improvement Association. Through their behavior, the Saints improved their standing in the eyes of many.

The influence of the war did not stop with the welcome-home parade in Salt Lake City. Throughout the conflict, leaders had been trained to assume positions of responsibility. The examples can be seen in soldiers' ecclesiastical and public service. The work of Major Richard W. Young and others had an international effect. Experiences during the Spanish-American War continued to affect the lives of Latter-day Saints for decades.

Soon after the battle-scarred veterans returned to Utah, the *Improvement Era* ran a brief article on the experiences of these men. Written by President Joseph F. Smith, this editorial shows a belief that God had protected the soldiers. "What has been termed good luck, but what rather must be recognized as the blessing of God, has accompanied the Utah boys in their travels, in their battles, in their return. Free from storms of nature, and troubles among men, their transports crossed the seas in peace. Notwithstanding they were constantly at the front, their number in killed and wounded is phenomenally small. Out of the three hundred and fifty-four enlisted, only thirteen have died. Thus the Almighty has marvelously preserved them from both the fire of the enemy and the ravages of disease."[65] In addition to these miraculous events, Latter-day Saint soldiers performed miracles on the battlefield that helped boost the reputation of the Church. The Church demonstrated in a remarkable way that service in the military during wartime was in the veins of its people. To all fair observers, it was clear that Latter-day Saints could be counted on to stand by their nation. Since then, the Church has never looked back.

Notes

1. See Journal History of the Church of Jesus Christ of Latter-day Saints, April 5, 1898, 2, Church Archives, The Church of Jesus Christ of Latter-day Saints, Salt Lake City.

2. See George J. A. O'Toole, *The Spanish American War: An American Epic* (New York: W. W. Norton, 1984), 12.

3. Not every soldier in the Utah units was a Latter-day Saint; however, members of the Church made up the majority of their numbers.

4. "Repeated efforts to obtain statehood had been made by Utahns since the conclusion of the Mexican War. Six proposed state constitutions (1849, 1856, 1862, 1872, 1882, 1887) had been submitted to Congress with petitions for statehood, only to be rejected or tabled indefinitely" (D. Michael Quinn, "The Mormon Church and the Spanish American War: An End to Selective Pacifism," in *Dialogue: A Journal of Mormon Thought* 17, no. 4 [Winter 1984], 21).

5. George Q. Cannon, in Conference Report, April 6, 1898, 9.

6. Brigham Young Jr., in Conference Report, April 7, 1898, 27.

7. See Brigham H. Roberts, in Conference Report, April 7, 1898, 27–28.

8. Francis M. Lyman, in Conference Report, April 8, 1898, 58.

9. See Joseph Smith Jr. as quoted in Wilford Woodruff, in Conference Report, April 7, 1898, 57. Like other Latter-day Saints, President Woodruff did think the Second Coming was at hand. In that same talk, he said, "I will say here that I shall not live to see it, you may not live to see it; but these thousands of Latter-day Saint children that belong to the Sabbath schools, I believe many of them will stand in the flesh when the Lord Jesus Christ visits the Zion of God here in the mountains of Israel."

10. Franklin D. Richards, in Conference Report, April 9, 1898, 82.

11. See George Q. Cannon, in Conference Report, April 9, 1898, 83–87.

12. Wilford Woodruff, in Conference Report, April 9, 1898, 89.

13. Woodruff, in Conference Report, April 9, 1898, 89.

14. Woodruff, in Conference Report, April 9, 1898, 89.

15. Woodruff, in Conference Report, April 9, 1898, 90.

16. Official Declaration 1, Excerpts from Three Addresses by President Wilford Woodruff Regarding the Manifesto.

17. See O'Toole, *Spanish American War*, 11–13; and Scott Kennedy, ed., *Wilford Woodruff's Journal, 1833–1898* (Midvale, UT: Signature Books, 1983–84), 9:546.

18. Young's feelings about yellow fever came from personal experience. As a member of the Quorum of the Twelve Apostles, his duty was to travel the globe preaching the gospel and shoring up the strength of the Saints. In 1882 he traveled to Mexico to visit the Yacqui Indians. While there he fell sick with yellow fever and almost died. Fortunately, he was healed by the power of God (see Andrew Jenson, *Latter-Day Saint Biographical Encyclopedia* [Salt Lake City: Deseret News, 1901], 1:121–26). Having experienced the awful effects of this illness, Young was not eager that his fellow Saints experience the same thing.

19. See Journal History, April 24, 1898, 2. "A truism well recognized by medical men is that the soldier has much more to fear from the ravages of disease than the fire of the enemy. . . . In the Spanish-American War there was only one death from battle to 12.5 deaths from disease" (J. E. Greaves, "Some Fundamentals of Health Conservation," *Improvement Era, 1918*, October 1918, 1051).

20. *Wilford Woodruff's Journal*, 9:546.

21. Quinn, "Mormon Church and the Spanish American War," 28.

22. See "The Mutual Improvement Association of the Far East" section of this chapter, p. 180.

23. See James R. Clark, ed., *Messages of the First Presidency* (Salt Lake City: Bookcraft, 1966), 3:298–99.

24. See Lowell E. Call, "Latter-day Saint Servicemen in the Philippine Islands: A Historical Study of Their Religious Activities and Influences

Resulting in the Official Organization of The Church of Jesus Christ of Latter-day Saints in the Philippines" (master's thesis, Brigham Young University, 1955), 86.

25. Call, "Latter-day Saint Servicemen in the Philippine Islands," 81.

26. Richard W. Young, "Mormons at Manila," in *Harper's Weekly*, March 25, 1899, 297.

27. See A. Prestiss, *The History of the Utah Volunteers in the Spanish-American War and in the Philippine Islands: A Complete History of All the Military Organizations in Which Utah Men Served* (n.p., n.d.), 29–30.

28. Nephi Jensen, "The Extremity," *Improvement Era*, April 1919, 525.

29. Journal of Elias Smith Kimball, June 14, 1898, 3–4, Church Archives, The Church of Jesus Christ of Latter-day Saints, Salt Lake City, UT.

30. Journal of Elias Smith Kimball, June 14, 1898; 192, 1–2.

31. Journal of Elias Smith Kimball, July 18, 1898, 60–61.

32. Journal of Elias Smith Kimball, July 26, 1898, 80–81.

33. See Journal of Elias Smith Kimball, July 24, 1898, 74–77.

34. Journal of Elias Smith Kimball, August 4, 1898, 103.

35. H. H. Caldwell, as quoted in O'Toole, *Spanish American War*, 174.

36. See O'Toole, *Spanish American War*, 192–93.

37. See Journal History, August 6, 1899, 6–7.

38. *Brigadier General Richard W. Young in Memoriam: Biographical Sketch, Funeral Ceremonies, Resolutions of Respect* (Salt Lake City: n.p., 1920), 13.

39. Journal History, August 6, 1899, 6–7.

40. See Charles R. Mabey, *The Utah Batteries: A History* (Salt Lake City: Daily Reporter, 1900), 16.

41. "It was Utah's distinction to have been the only state that had men in those trenches every night during the siege, owing to the fact that Utah furnished the only available artillery in the corps" (Richard W. Young, "Last Hours of Dr. Harry A. Young," *Improvement Era*, July 1899, 643).

42. J. D. Mitchell, *Song Book for Soldiers* (n.p., 1898), PAM 14675, Utah State Historical Society Library, Salt Lake City, song 5.

43. Journal History, August 5, 1899.

44. See B. H. Roberts, *A Comprehensive History of the Church of Jesus Christ of Latter-day Saints* (Salt Lake City: Deseret News, 1930), 6:458.

45. Scrapbooks full of newspaper clippings about the Spanish-American War can be found in the Richard W. Young Papers, MS 104, Box 8, Book 5, Special Collections, University of Utah, Salt Lake City.

46. B. H. Roberts, "Progress of the War between Spain and the United States of America," *Improvement Era*, December 1898, 131.

47. George Seaman, "The 'Far East' Improvement Association," *Improvement Era*, December 1898, 152.

48. See Seaman, "The 'Far East' Improvement Association," 154; and Call, "Latter-day Saint Servicemen in the Philippine Islands," 92–97.

49. Mabey, *The Utah Batteries*, 30. Mabey does speak of other activities that helped the soldiers pass the time. For example, the organizations within the Eighth Army Corps each had their own baseball team. Utah played many of the other states, but in the end "Utah carried the trophy away to America."

50. Call, "Latter-day Saint Serviceman in the Philippine Islands," 85. However, R. Lanier Britsch reports that both of these men were set apart by Elder John Henry Smith (*From the East: The History of the Latter-day Saints in Asia, 1851–1996* [Salt Lake City: Deseret Book, 1998], 318–19).

51. Call, "Latter-day Saint Servicemen in the Philippine Islands," 98.

52. Appropriately enough, these two men had been set apart by Apostles, whose prerogative it is "to build up the church, and regulate all the affairs of the same in all nations" (D&C 107:33).

53. Louis Paul Murray, "The Life of Brigadier General W. Young" (master's thesis, University of Utah, 1959), 108.

54. Murray, "The Life of Brigadier General W. Young," 114–18.

55. Heber J. Grant, *Gospel Standards: Selections from the Sermons and Writings of Heber J. Grant*, comp. G. Homer Durham (Salt Lake City: Improvement Era, 1981), 272. President Grant also shared the following: "I rejoice in having had ex-President Taft say to me when I met him upon

a trip to Washington: 'Mr. Grant, you did not call on me the last time you were here. Now I want it understood that you are never to come to Washington without coming to see me. There is in my heart a warm feeling for your people. I have great respect for them, and I want you to call on me whenever you are here'" (*Gospel Standards*, 90).

56. Mabey, *The Utah Batteries*, 32.

57. Prestiss, *History of the Utah Volunteers*, 128.

58. Prestiss, *History of the Utah Volunteers*, 131.

59. See Mabey, *The Utah Batteries*, 99–100.

60. See "Events of the Month," *Improvement Era*, January 1904, 395.

61. See Andrew Jenson, *Church Chronology: A Record of Important Events Pertaining to the History of the Church of Jesus Christ of Latter-day Saints* (Salt Lake City: Deseret News, 1914), 19.

62. *R. W. Young in Memoriam*, 14.

63. Richard L. Evans, in Conference Report, April 1950, 105.

64. Prestiss, *History of the Utah Volunteers*, 30–31.

65. Joseph F. Smith, "Editor's Table," *Improvement Era*, September 1899, 87.

Index

A

Allen, James, 42–47, 54
Armageddon, 5
Assyrians, 14

B

Babbitt, Almon W., 93
Ballard, Melvin J., 186
Battle of the Bulls, 62–63
"Battle Song of Utah," 177–78
Beauregard, Pierre G. T., 109
Bennett, John C., 28
Benson, Ezra Taft, 16
Bigler, Henry William, 65
Bjarnson, Stephen, 166

"Bleeding Kansas," 78, 92–93, 98, 119
Boley, Samuel, 50
Boyle, Henry, 68
Boynton, John, 24
Bragg, Braxton, 38
Brown, James S., 51, 60
Buchanan, James, 78, 85, 93
Bull Run, battles of, 109
Burnside, Ambrose, 109
Burton, Robert T., 132–35
Butler, Benjamin F., 110

C

Call, Willard, 166, 182–83
Camp Crittenden, 94, 103
Camp Douglas, 140

Camp Floyd, 94, 103, 140
Cannon, George Q., 157, 160, 164
Cervera, Pascual, 153
Chaplains, Latter-day Saint, 167–72, 187
Civil War, 22, casualties, 115; causes of, 107–8; end of, 111; prophecies of, 115–16, 118–19
Cleveland, Grover, 152
Comaduran, Don Antonio, 64
Connor, Patrick Edward, 139
Constitution, U.S., 18, 142, 163
Cooke, Philip St. George, 48–49, 58–59, 94
Crismon, Charles, Jr., 137
Crittenden-Johnson Resolution, 109
Crosby, William, 55–56
Cuba: fights for independence, 152, 156; granted independence, 154; naval blockade, 152; Santiago de Cuba attacked, 153
Cumming, Alfred, 99, 147

D

David, King, 7–8
Davies, Benjamin, 129
Davis, Jefferson, 38
Dewey, George, 153, 172–73
Doniphan, Alexander W., 57–58
Douglas, Stephen A., 93, 124–25, 144–45
Drummond, William W., 93
Dusenberry, Harvey, 176–77

E

Enoch, 8, 21
Evans, John Davis, 121–22

F

Floyd, John B., 94, 98
Ford, Thomas, 30
Fort Bridger, 102
Fort Douglas, 183
Fort Leavenworth, Kansas, 43
Foster, Stephen Clark, 64
Founding Fathers, 162

G

God: as perfect Judge, 15; eternal perspective of, 20; "man of war," 13; respects agency, 21; turns war to good purposes, 18
Gold Rush, California, 65
Goodwin, C. C., 178–79
Grant, Frank A., 174–75

Grant, Jedediah M., 27, 116
Grant, Ulysses S., 109–10
Guam, 154

H

Hancock, Levi, 53, 61
Harney, William, 98
Haun's Mill, 25–26
Hay, John, 151
Herrera, Jose Joaquin, 36
Hinckley, Gordon B., 4, 9
Hitler, Adolf, 15
Hooker, Joseph, 109
Hooper, William Henry, 146–47
Hullinger, Harvey C., 137
Hunt, Jefferson, 52–54
Hurt, Garland, 93

I

Independence, Missouri, 24
Isolationism, 156–57

J

Jackson, Henry Wells, 142
Jennings, Frank, 178
John the Revelator, 4
Johnson, Luke, 24
Johnston's army. *See* Utah War

Johnston, Albert Sidney, 94, 97, 99, 102, 122, 146
Johnston, Joseph E., 109

K

Kane, Thomas L., 100–101, 103
Kearny, Stephen W., 42, 58
Kimball, Elias, 167–72, 185, 187
Kimball, J. Golden, 169
Kimball, Spencer W., 7, 13
Kirtland, Ohio, conflicts, 23–24

L

Law of warfare, 12
Lee, Harold B., 19–20
Lee, Robert E., 107, 109–10
Lincoln, Abraham, 108, and Latter-day Saints, 123–26

M

Mabey, Charles R., 183, 185
Maine, USS, 152, 155, 157
Manila, U.S. attack on, 154
Marcy, William L., 41
Marshall, James, 65
Martí, José, 152
McClellan, George, 109
McIntyre, William L., 55
McKay, David O., 8, 11–12

McKinley, William, 155–56, 162, 169
Meade, George, 110
Meranda, J. W., 175
Mexican-American War: causes of, 35; Church and, 41–44; end of, 39; Mormon Battalion mustered in, 45–45
Michael, Archangel, 2–3, 5
Miles, Nelson, 154
Mining in Utah, 140–41
Mississippi Saints, 55
Missouri: Haun's Mill, 25–26; Jackson County, 6
Mormon Battalion: fights Battle of the Bulls, 62–63; in Cimarron Desert, 57; in Imperial Desert, 67; in San Diego, 69; Indians befriend, 64, 66; money donated to Saints, 51–52; mustered in, 44–45; mustered out, 68, 70; sick detachments, 56–61; skirmish near Tucson, 64; women and children with, 50
Moroni, 19
Moroni, Captain, 9–11
Mountain Meadows Massacre, 79, 83–84
Mutual Improvement Association of the Far East, 180–82

N

Native Americans, Church policy toward, 90, 96
Nauvoo, Illinois, 28
Nauvoo Legion, 28–31, 95

P

Paredes y Arrillaga, Mariano, 36
Parrish, Warren, 24
Patten, David W., 116–17
Peery, David Harold, 130
Petersen, Andrew, 175
Philippines: attacked by U.S. forces, 153; purchased from Spain, 154
Polk, James K., 36–37, 41
Pratt, Orson, 118–19
Puerto Rico: attacked, 154; ceded to United States, 154

R

Rawlins, Joseph, 155
Red Cross, 184
Reshaw, John, 55–56
Revolutionary War, 16–17, 162
Rex, William, 123
Richards, Franklin D., 116, 160, 171
Rigdon, Sidney, 27
Roberts, B. H., 158

S

Sanderson, George B., 54
Santa Anna, Antonio López de, 36–39
Satan: influence on wars, 3
Scott, Winfield, 94, 98
Seaman, George, 180, 182
Seven Days' Campaign, 109
Seward, William H., 108
Shafter, William, 153–54
Sharp, Thomas, 30
Sheridan, Philip H., 111
Sherman, William Tecumseh, 111
Slidell, John, 36–37
Smith, Andrew Jackson, 48–49, 54
Smith, Joseph: on slavery, 143; on war, 21–22, 115–16, 118–19, 126, 141
Smith, Joseph F., 18, 161, 188
Smith, Lot, 82, 102, 135–39
Smith, William F., 110
Smoot, Reed, 178
South Carolina, secession of, 108
Spain, fight for independence from, 151–54
Spanish-American War: causes of, 151–53; U.S. declares war, 162
states' rights, 107
Stoneman, George, 48, 58
Sutter, John, 65

T

Taft, William Howard, 183
telegraph, first overland, 131
terrorist attacks, 4
Tyler, Daniel, 55, 63

U

Utah artillery batteries, 165–66, 173–79
Utah Expedition. *See* Utah War
Utah Volunteers, 187
Utah War: and states' rights, 78; causes of, 77–78, 90, 119; end of, 103–4; impact on Church, 82–83, 104

V

Van Vliet, Stewart, 98

W

War: conditions justifying, 11–12, 166; defensive, 9, 11, 31; in heaven, 3; Lord's view, 5; need to proclaim peace, 6–7; origins of, 3; pronouncements on, 157–62; Satan's role in, 3, 164; sign of last days, 22
Washington, George, 17, 162

Webster, Daniel, 35
Wells, Daniel H., 136
Wells, Daniel, 95
Wilcken, Charles Henry, 88
Woodruff, Wilford, 43, 158–62, 163–64

Y

Young, Brigham, 28, and cotton mission, 128–29; and Mormon Battalion, 42–44, 70–71; and Utah War, 78–79; first overland telegraph message of, 131–32; isolationist views, 88
Young, Brigham, Jr., 157–58, 163–64
Young, Richard W., 164, 174–75, 180, 182–83, 185–86
Young, Willard, 164, 170

Z

Zion's Camp, 25–27

About the Editor

ROBERT C. FREEMAN

Robert C. Freeman is director of the Saints at War project at Brigham Young University. This publication is a direct result of his and other scholars' research into the experience of Latter-day Saints during wartime. In two previous volumes, both published by Covenant Communications, Freeman and colleague Dennis Wright have focused on the experiences of Latter-day Saints during World War II, the Korean War, and the Vietnam War. The present volume is a collaborative effort involving several scholars, including David F. Boone, Sherman L. Fleek, James I. Mangum, Larry C. Porter, and Andrew C. Skinner.